SHAKESPEARE FOR ALL

Volume 1

THE PRIMARY SCHOOL

An Account of the RSA Shakespeare in Schools Project

Also available from Cassell:

P. Ainley: *Young People Leaving Home*
P. Ainley and M. Corney: *Training for the Future: The Rise and Fall of the Manpower Services Commission*
G. Antonouris and J. Wilson: *Equal Opportunities in Schools*
L. Bash and D. Coulby: *Contradiction and Conflict in Education: The 1988 Act in Action*
N. Bennett and A. Cass: *From Special to Ordinary Schools*
D. E. Bland: *Managing Higher Education*
M. Booth, J. Furlong and M. Wilkin: *Partnership in Initial Teacher Training*
M. Bottery: *The Morality of the School*
L. Burton (ed.): *Gender and Mathematics*
C. Christofi: *Assessment and Profiling in Science*
G. Claxton: *Being a Teacher: A Positive Approach to Change and Stress*
G. Claxton: *Teaching to Learn: A Direction for Education*
D. Coulby and L. Bash: *The Education Reform Act: Competition and Control*
D. Coulby and S. Ward: *The Primary Core National Curriculum*
C. Cullingford (ed.): *The Primary Teacher*
L. B. Curzon: *Teaching in Further Education* (4th edition)
J. Freeman: *Gifted Children Grow Up*
B. Goacher *et al.*: *Policy and Provision for Special Educational Needs*
H. Gray (ed.): *Management Consultancy in Schools*
L. Hall: *Poetry for Life*
J. Nias, G. Southworth and R. Yeomans: *Staff Relationships in the Primary School*
A. Pollard: *The Social World of the Primary School*
J. Sayer and V. Williams (eds): *Schools and External Relations*
B. Spiecker and R. Straughan: *Freedom and Indoctrination in Education: International Perspectives*
R. Straughan: *Beliefs, Behaviour and Education*
H. Thomas: *Education Costs and Performance*
H. Thomas, G. Kirkpatrick and E. Nicholson: *Financial Delegation and the Local Management of Schools*
D. Thyer and J. Maggs: *Teaching Mathematics to Young Children* (3rd edition)
M. Watts: *The Science of Problem-Solving*
J. Wilson: *A New Introduction to Moral Education*
S. Wolfendale (ed.): *Parental Involvement*
S. Wolfendale *et al.* (eds): *The Profession and Practice of Educational Psychology*

Shakespeare for All

Volume 1

The Primary School

An Account of the RSA Shakespeare in Schools Project

Edited by

Maurice Gilmour

'*People think Shakespeare is posh and serious, but when we did it, it was fun.*'
(John aged 9)

CASSELL

Cassell

Wellington House
125 Strand
London WC2R OBB

PO Box 605
Herndon
VA 20172

First published in 1997

British Library Cataloguing-in-Publication Data

A catalogue record for this book is available from the British Library.

ISBN 0-304-33791-9 (hardback)
      0-304-33792-7 (paperback)

Printed and bound in Great Britain by Redwood Books, Trowbridge, Wiltshire

Front cover: Portrait of Lady Macbeth (pupil aged 9, Markfield Mercenfeld Primary)

Contents

Palmer, Anne Watts, Janet Thomas, Sue Gammon, Lynne Grindlay, Juliet Gasser, Elspeth Myles, Sue Trigg, Katherine Liggins, Clare Mulholland and Patsy Ryder

Participating Schools

(Staff named are those who participated in the Project.)

AVENUE JUNIOR SCHOOL Head Teacher: Frank Gallagher

Staff: Ian North, Dorothy Waite, Carol James, Margot Fawcett, Helen Loydall, Pat Bastock, Vivienne Walthoe, Jim Campbell, Amanda Roberts, Deborah Hardy, Kenneth Wheatley, Caroline Roper, Yvonne Addison, Terri Deal, Sue Massey, Linda Billam

Avenue Junior is an inner-city school in Leicester and has 320 pupils aged 7 to 11. The socio-economic range of families is as wide as is likely to be found in any primary school. The school building is a large late Victorian chalet-bungalow, the focal point of which is a grand hall, panelled, balconied with a magnificent clerestory and a hammer-beamed wooden ceiling. This is surrounded by classrooms which open off the hall. This comparatively large school has many of the positive characteristics of the small village schoolroom. A large 'family' and 'sharing' ethos is easy to maintain.

COLEMAN PRIMARY SCHOOL Head Teacher: John Adams

Staff: Ed Farrow, Rhiannon Jenkins, Beverley Hodges

Coleman Primary School is situated towards the centre of Leicester, serving a mixed social, economic housing area. There are 550 pupils on roll between ages 5–11 and a further 120 in the nursery. The majority of the children are bilingual (about 75 per cent), so many will speak Gujerati,

Punjabi or Hindi at home and English at school. Because of cultural differences the children of some faiths are not permitted to perform in public (although many children will perform in class plays). In addition there are strong allegiances to supplementary schools which take place in the evenings. This led, for example, to us rehearsing three Quinces for various performances – for sometimes we had very, very short notice that a child was unavailable.

ELIZABETH WOODVILLE PRIMARY SCHOOL Head Teacher: Tony Gil

Staff: Anne Hitchins

Elizabeth Woodville is an open-plan school with 234 children on roll. Built in the early seventies, it mainly serves the village of Groby on the outskirts of the City of Leicester. When children leave Elizabeth Woodville they go on to study at Brookvale High and then Groby Community College.

KIRBY MUXLOE PRIMARY SCHOOL Head Teacher: Mr B. M. Thompson

Staff: Linda Weir, Sue Freeman, Ann Palmer, Anne Watts, Janet Thomas, Sue Gammon, Lynne Grindlay, Juliet Gasser, Elspeth Myles, Sue Trigg, Katherine Liggins, Clare Mulholland, Patsy Ryder

Kirby Muxloe Primary School is located in the centre of the village of Kirby Muxloe, a largely residential area on the outskirts of the City of Leicester. The school's catchment area largely comprises private housing, although there is a small council development in the village. The school was built in 1910. The accommodation includes eleven classrooms, library, technology room and swimming pool. There are 285 pupils on roll, rising to 315 in the summer term. The school is an important feature of the local community and benefits from strong parental support.

LADY JANE GREY PRIMARY SCHOOL Head Teacher: Julia Beckreck

Staff: Victoria Higgins

Lady Jane Grey is the most recent primary school built to serve the expanding village of Groby. It is a very modern, open-plan building and presently has 101 children on roll.

ST PETER'S C OF E PRIMARY SCHOOL, MARKET BOSWORTH
Head Teacher: Mrs Annie Webster

Staff: Andrew Chapman, Gill Edwards, Paul Abell, Alwyn Whitney, Jean Wasteney, Pat Glasscock, Philippa Hodgetts, Liz George, Jan Sparrow, Sue Simpson.

St Peter's Primary School has 250 children on roll. Built in 1975, the school is situated in the town of Market Bosworth surrounded by attractive countryside and places of historic interest, including the site of the Battle of Bosworth Field. The building has been enlarged and now includes nine classrooms, a studio, a resource room and a library.

Classes are mainly mixed-ability and vertically grouped. The organization and content of the curriculum are planned with the emphasis on individual learning.

MARTINSHAW PRIMARY SCHOOL Head Teacher: Steve White

Staff: Joy Walton, Di Watson, John Gillingham, Chris Heley

Martinshaw Primary School was built in the late fifties and serves the village of Groby. The original village school was overcrowded, so this school, built in the traditional style, replaced it over a period of years.

Like many villages of its type, Groby has grown enormously over the past thirty years and now has three primary schools. There are 195 pupils on roll in Martinshaw. The catchment area includes both private and rented accommodation, with families from a wide socio-economic range.

MERCENFELD PRIMARY SCHOOL Head Teacher: John Kitchen

Staff: Elizabeth Lamb, Andrew Cotton, Anthony Squires, Sarah Elsey

Mercenfeld Primary is a 4+ to 10+ school in Markfield, in the North of Leicestershire. There are 205 children on roll. Markfield, an expanding village, serves as a dormitory for the majority of parents who work in Leicester and its environs. The school was originally in the heart of the village but moved to its present modern site some fifteen years ago. There is a mixture of housing within the catchment area.

NEWTOWN LINFORD PRIMARY SCHOOL Head Teacher: Mrs S. M. Foster

Staff: David Ashfield, Margaret Hardwicke, Sian Mollart, Sheila Langton, Hilary Horricks.

Newtown Linford is a small village adjacent to Bradgate Park, the well known country park. The school, which serves a rural area, has around 70 children. These are divided into three classes, Reception and Year 1, Years 2, 3 and 4 and Years 5 and 6. As our school only has three classrooms, a library and office we use the local village hall for games, dance and drama. This is where the TIE production of *Macbeth* took place. In the past we have also had a summer production on the grassy area next to the playground (far too small to be called a field!).

RATBY PRIMARY SCHOOL Head Teacher: Mrs G. E. Lewis

Staff: Anne Joyce

Ratby Primary School has 292 children on roll, ages rising 5 to 11 years. It mainly serves the rural village of Ratby which is situated on the outskirts of Leicester. The original school building is Victorian but two modern additions to the school were constructed in the 1970s and 1980s.

STAFFORD LEYS PRIMARY SCHOOL Head Teacher: Chris Meadows

Staff: Helen Boot, Glyn Millinchip, Granville Rushton, Angela Guiver

Stafford Leys is a Group 2 school with 302 pupils. The school was opened in 1966 and extended in 1975 with the addition of an open-plan extension and a second hall. The school has six closed classrooms and five classes in an open-plan area. Stafford Leys is classified as a four plus school, so that children within the school's catchment area are able to begin school at the age of four years as long as their birthday is before 1 September in the year of entry. Pupils leave at the end of Year 5 to go to the High School. The catchment area is made up of a variety of private housing.

STANTON UNDER BARDON PRIMARY SCHOOL
Head Teacher: Steve Winter

Staff: Steve Winter

The school mainly serves the small village of Stanton Under Bardon in North West Leicestershire. There are 58 children on roll. The school has been largely re-built after the discovery of dry rot in the timbers of the original village school. For a year the children and staff occupied a corner of a large, empty new primary school on the outskirts of the City of Leicester, having to be bussed there and back every day. They are now back in their refurbished village school.

THORNTON PRIMARY SCHOOL Head Teacher: Elise Watchorn

Staff: Muriel Walker

Thornton Primary is a co-educational school for 4–10 year olds. The present school was opened in 1881 and extended in 1910. Substantial redevelopment took place between 1983 and 1985. The number on roll is 100. The children are divided into four classes and come from a mixed catchment area.

Acknowledgements

(The following have all been closely involved in the development of the project and have made a major contribution. Between the end of the Project and the publication of the materials, some have moved on or retired, but the positions indicated were those held while the project was taking place. *Editor*)

RSA: ROYAL SOCIETY FOR ARTS MANUFACTURES AND COMMERCE

Andrew Fairbairn	Chairman, Arts Advisory Group
Antony Holloway	Chairman, East Midlands Committee
Christopher Lucas	Director
Penny Egan	Arts Secretary
Elizabeth Winder	Administrative Assistant

ROYAL SHAKESPEARE COMPANY

Tony Hill	Projects Director
Wendy Greenhill	Head of Education

HAYMARKET THEATRE, LEICESTER

John Blackmore	Executive Director
Julia Bardsley	Artistic Director

DE MONTFORT UNIVERSITY

Prof. Michael Scott	Associate Director and Head of Arts
Peter Walden	Dean of Education
Joan Stephenson	Lecturer in Education
Jane Dowson	Lecturer in Education
Roger Stranwick	Lecturer in Education
Elizabeth Grugeon	Lecturer in Education

LEICESTERSHIRE LOCAL EDUCATION AUTHORITY

Keith Wood-Allum	Director of Education
Maurice Gilmour	General Adviser, Drama and Dance
Cherry Stephenson	Acting head of Drama and Dance Advisory
Rick Lee	Advisory Teacher for Drama

KEYSTAGE THEATRE IN EDUCATION COMPANY

Paul Waring	Senior Actor/Teacher
Jane Perkins	Actor/Teacher
Simon Cuckson	Actor/Teacher
Ruth Hellier	Actor/Teacher
Peter Jackson	Technical Director
Maurice Gilmour	Director

SPONSORS

Calouste Gulbenkian Foundation
East Midlands Arts
Edward Boyle Memorial Trust
Jerwood Foundation
Leicestershire Appeal for Music and the Arts
Leicestershire Co-operative Society Ltd
Paul Hamlyn Foundation
Prince Charles' Charitable Trust
Reed International plc
Weetabix Ltd

Foreword

There has been a tendency in the past thirty years or so to 'interpret' in simple terms many of the great classics of literature, liturgy and music. Very often Shakespeare has not been 'interpreted', but simply ditched – there must be a moral in this! All sorts of reasons are given by the protagonists of 'interpretation' – study of the original would be too difficult, too elitist, not sexy enough and in any case the new generation are mainly visually conscious and have to be led gradually to the classics. In some measure this dilution of original, classical works has been due to the difficult transitions from selective (11+) secondary to comprehensive secondary education. When only 25 per cent of all children were selected for grammar schools, the tendency was to confine Shakespeare to the 'sheep' and deny the 'goats' the opportunity because the Bard was not suitable for the lower abilities. What nonsense! Expectations were not high enough and in some measure this has permeated some comprehensives, even though most have opened the doors to at least 40 per cent of the age group.

The contention of this Project is that Shakespeare is accessible *in the original* to all age groups from 5 upwards provided that the teaching and learning approach is well prepared and made exciting and enjoyable. We sought to demonstrate that the approaches set out in this book are applicable to the smallest rural primary school and also to similarly situated secondary comprehensives. The remarkable spontaneity and relish with which all ages of youngster studied – and performed – *The Dream, Macbeth* and *Romeo and Juliet,* to name but a few, demonstrated to me that it is quite wrong to deny to our youngsters the experience of the magnificent language, the wisdom, the history and the humanity of everyday living enshrined in the works of the Bard. I hope this book will inspire others to have a go, too.

Andrew N. Fairbairn
Former Director of Education for Leicestershire and
Chairman of the RSA Advisory Arts Group

Background to the RSA Shakespeare Project

In 1992, the Advisory Arts Group of the ROYAL SOCIETY OF ARTS MANUFACTURES AND COMMERCE (RSA), chaired by Andrew Fairbairn, identified key issues related to the arts in education, and agreed on the need to:

- Highlight the value of the arts in the curriculum.
- Improve access to the arts for all school pupils.
- Inspire confidence in teachers to deal with a wide spectrum of the arts, including those sometimes thought to be difficult because of historical content or technical or intellectual complexity. (In the 1982 Gulbenkian report *The Arts in Schools* these were called 'the high arts'.)
- Promulgate good practice among head teachers, governors, politicians and policy makers.
- Give a focus to the arts at a time when they are under threat from underfunding and weakly represented within the National Curriculum.

After a period of consultation, it was decided to focus on one aspect of the arts and consider its application within a small group of schools. From the particular, it was hoped that general conclusions could be drawn. The RSA adopted a project proposed by Leicestershire Education Authority in association with a family of schools based around Groby Community College on the outskirts of Leicester. The schools offered to undertake and evaluate a programme of teaching that would **introduce Shakespeare to pupils of all abilities and all age ranges from 5 to 18 years.** They aimed to show that Shakespeare offers a wealth of educational experiences for all pupils, given appropriate teaching methods, and charges that his plays are too difficult, boring, irrelevant or inaccessible are the result of a method of teaching that satisfies only an academic and analytical need. Not that they sought to refute this method; on the contrary, it was agreed that scholarship is to be nurtured, but that it also needs to be complemented by other teaching approaches. Teachers thought strongly that Shakespeare ought not to be seen as a bogeyman to be faced on entering secondary school, but should be a familiar and welcome figure from a very early age. It was not their intention, however, to promote Shakespeare as a daily or weekly or even monthly curriculum subject area, but to consider the possibility of pupils being engaged in a Shakespeare play at every Key Stage from the age of 5 through an approach that was challenging, enjoyable, meaningful and relevant. If pupils enter secondary education having had favourable contact with Shakespeare's plays at primary level, would it not help them and their teachers? Would an attitude of enjoyable expectation not be preferable to one of trepidation and disinterest?

> Hello, I'm Mark. My best part of Midsummer Night's Dream is what I'm doing. This is it, I'm playing the courtiers walking up the aisle. I'm a wall in a house and after a few minutes I'll be a lovely tree and then a bunch of horrid trees. Then I turn into a goblin and pounce around the bunch of trees like a bunch of zombies. I jump like an elf through two lazy trees. They have got a big hole through the middle of the trees. I would like to show our play to loads of people.
>
> (Pupil, aged 8, Thornton Primary)

A Steering Committee set up by the schools and chaired by Philip Watson, Principal of Groby Community College, set down the following aims for the Project:

1. To demonstrate that studying Shakespeare can be an enjoyable activity.
2. To demonstrate that Shakespeare's plays can be made accessible to students of all abilities from 5 to 18.
3. To demonstrate that a variety of approaches are available and have validity.
4. To demonstrate that his plays and themes can be used across the curriculum.
5. To demonstrate that students can come to an understanding of text both as literature and through performance.
6. To produce resource materials which can be made available to other teachers.
7. To encourage collaboration between schools and teachers through activities such as INSET.
8. To disseminate the evaluation of the Project to a national audience.

One of the interesting and useful aspects of the Steering Committee was the meeting together of staff from primary and secondary schools to plan the detail of the Project. Since a central aim was to look at the continuity of experience from 5 to 18 years, the meetings provided an excellent framework for exchanging ideas and exploring common ground.

The schools included Groby Community College with pupils aged 14–18 and a community remit, two high schools for pupils aged 11–14 years, one high school for pupils aged 10–14 years and thirteen primary schools with pupils aged 4–10 or 4–11 years. The primary schools varied from a small village school with 60 pupils to a large inner-city with more than 600. The practical work took place from September 1992 to March 1993. Most of it was classroom based, but it included formal productions. Teachers received varying degrees of classroom support from Cherry Stephenson, acting head of Leicestershire drama and dance advisory service, and Rick Lee, advisory teacher for drama.

The RSA retained an overview of the Project through Andrew Fairbairn, Chairman of the RSA Arts Advisory Group; Christopher Lucas, Director of the RSA; Penny Egan, the RSA Arts Secretary; and Antony Holloway, Chairman of the RSA East Midlands' Regional Committee.

Professional support was provided by a number of agencies. Leicestershire LEA drama and dance advisory service gave practical classroom support and co-ordinated the Project, the Royal Shakespeare Company (RSC) and the Haymarket Theatre delivered practical, professional workshops on the language of Shakespeare, Keystage Theatre in Education Company presented and evaluated a performance of *Macbeth* in the primary schools, and De Montfort University evaluated two teaching programmes from each of the Key Stages. The work of visiting teachers, lecturers and professionals gave teachers opportunities to develop skills and ideas, to re-assess the potential of their pupils and to clarify the outcomes of the Project through a formal evaluation process.

Finance was needed to meet the costs of in-service training, the support provided by the external agencies, and collaborative activities. The schools and the Local Education Authority could commit staff, buildings, and other resources, but they were no longer in a position to provide hard cash. Local government finances were shrinking and schools were only then beginning to cope with the management of their own budgets. Yet 1992 was not the best time in which to seek sponsorship. It is to the credit of the RSA, particularly Andrew Fairbairn and Penny Egan, with strong encouragement from Simon Richey, Assistant Director of the Calouste Gulbenkian Foundation, that sufficient funding arrived to get the Project under way. The arts organizations, charitable institutions and businesses who gave generous support to the Project included:

The Calouste Gulbenkian Foundation
LAMA (The Leicestershire Appeal for Music and the Arts)
East Midlands Arts
The Edward Boyle Memorial Trust
The Sir John Stratton Fund
Reed International
The Jerwood Foundation
Leicester Co-operative Society
Weetabix

The Project also received enthusiastic support and a donation from the Prince Charles Private Charitable Trust. This coincided with the appointment of Prince Charles as President of the RSC and the establishment in Stratford of a summer school on teaching Shakespeare.

An important focal point was a Festival held from 9 to 12 March 1993 on the campus shared by Brookvale High and Groby Community College. This Festival acted as a shop window for the rich variety of work, and demonstrated the strength and purposefulness that can result from close collaboration between schools. It included an exhibition of children's writing, painting, and 3D designs. The library in Brookvale High was transformed into the Forest of Arden with foliage and lighting, and the exhibition was seen, as it were, in a succession of glades. The effect was magical and set off to great advantage the extensive and beautifully displayed range of written work, painted portraits or clay figures of characters from Shakespeare, photographs, and models based on scenes from his plays. Art work was also exhibited in Groby Community College.

Demonstrations of class work in drama, dance and music and formal productions were presented in Groby Community College every evening, culminating in Key Stage Theatre's presentation of their adaptation of *Macbeth* which had been toured to primary schools and evaluated as part of the Project.

During the week, teachers met for a day to share their ideas and experiences. This interchange between teachers in primary and secondary schools highlighted similar teaching problems and emphasized the importance of continuity of learning. The teachers from the secondary schools strongly supported the notion of a continuous experience of Shakespeare from the age of 5, so that pupils come to the work in the secondary school with a sense of enjoyment and anticipation. All agreed that the division into primary and secondary is not necessarily beneficial, and that methods applied by primary school teachers are also appropriate in the secondary schools, and vice versa.

The accounts of the work in the secondary schools form the main part of *Shakespeare for All in Secondary Schools*. That book includes details of the RSC workshops conducted by Wendy Greenhill of the RSC, including an adapted script of *Richard III*, and an account of the workshop on Shakespeare's language directed by John Blackmore of the Haymarket Theatre Leicester.

Chapter 1

Shakespeare in the Primary School: Introduction

Maurice Gilmour

For many years, Shakespeare has been an integral part of English literature exam-inations at 16 and beyond and, as such, is part of the education experience of many, though not all pupils in secondary school. This position changed radically with the introduction of the National Curriculum. From 1992, it became com-pulsory for teachers in Key Stages 3 and 4 to study the text of at least one Shake-speare play with all their pupils.

Although the subject of much debate, the general consensus is that Shake-speare's place within the English Literature curriculum is justified both by his qualities as a writer and the esteem in which he is held throughout the world. It is difficult to refute this. His output was prodigious, and his plays contain a wide and complex range of human relationships and situations. The language, rich in im-agery and dramatic power, moves fluently from heroic verse to the broad humour of the street. His plays are read and performed in many languages and have been turned into ballets, operas, music scores, films and cartoons; some, close inter-pretations of the original text, others, revised as contemporary parallels.

> Many teachers believe that Shakespeare's work conveys universal values, and that his language expresses rich and subtle meanings beyond that of any other English writer. Other teachers point out that evaluations of Shakespeare have varied from one historical period to the next, and they argue that pupils should be encouraged to think critically about his status in the canon. But almost everyone agrees that his work should be represented in a National Curriculum. Shakespeare's plays are so rich that in every age they can produce fresh meanings and even those who deny his universality agree on his cultural importance.
>
> (*The Cox Report: English for ages 5 to 16*, June 1989)

Given that Shakespeare commands such a high position in English and world literature, that he wrote in times when England was developing into a major world power, and that his plays have survived and been enjoyed through four centuries, it is not surprising that the literary justification is reinforced by the belief that he should be appreciated as part of England's historical tradition. On 9 September

1992, the then Education Secretary, John Patten, said, 'It is essential that pupils are encouraged to develop an understanding and appreciation of our country's literary heritage. Studying the works of Shakespeare is central to that development. That is why the study of Shakespeare is an explicit requirement of the National Curriculum.' At a time when social, economic and political patterns are changing swiftly and radically, a figure such as Shakespeare offers a secure link to the past as well as a rich educational experience.

However, he does present problems in the classroom. Not least of these is the complexity of the language and language patterns. Much that he wrote is in verse. Meaning can be obscured by archaic words and expressions, and by different usage of grammar and punctuation. Puns and topical references meant much more to the Elizabethan than to the modern reader. The plays were written for the stage, often for a particular set of circumstances, and were meant to be spoken aloud by professional actors. Not only do the teacher and class have to seek out the meaning of textual references, in order to experience the language in all its richness; they also need to speak the words. The complexity and length of many speeches can be daunting, requiring a high level of verbal fluency. Nor may the situations or characters appear immediately relevant to the modern student. Only by exploring the plays in some depth does the universality of the themes become clear and we find that the struggle for the crown in *Macbeth* reflects the power struggle that takes place in contemporary politics, on the sports' field, at home and in the school playground.

Traditionally, Shakespeare's plays have been approached mainly in secondary schools and as literature, involving an academic appreciation of the language and imagery, and an assessment of the characters and their relationships. Rarely is any practical work involved. Although this can be an enjoyable and educational experience, it is a limited approach. Alternative practical approaches, which still involve academic research and appreciation, may establish stronger links between the play and the experience of the pupils. The plays of Shakespeare are rich and full in stories, characters, situations, language, wit, bawdiness, humour, action, colour, pageantry, romance, lust, mystery, magic and music. They explore the major themes of life which are common to us all, the pursuit of position, power, love and happiness. The dilemma is how to make them accessible, and accessible to *all* pupils, not just those who are academically inclined.

If pupils do not meet Shakespeare until faced with a full text as part of a GCSE course, many will have problems of reading, speaking or understanding. They are suddenly confronted by a world inhabited by aristocrats speaking in blank verse and using incomprehensible images, and so-called clowns who tell very unfunny jokes.

Another dilemma facing teachers in secondary school is the nature of examinations, which do not require any evidence of pupil development, but concentrate mainly on an academic and literary response. Students are expected to appreciate the form and content of a play and to express their views in essay form, supporting argument with textual reference and quotations. This role of literary critic is one which the vast majority gladly surrender once they have left school, perceiving Shakespeare as a school task which has nothing to do with the mainstream of life. Teachers often lack experience of teaching Shakespeare except through a desk-bound approach and, like their pupils, may find Shakespeare difficult and not relevant to modern-day life; those who would like to adopt a more active approach are often hampered by the physical problem of class size and space.

These constraints have resulted in a tendency to restrict access to those pupils capable of detailed textual analysis and with good verbal and written skills.

Although Shakespeare is a requirement of the National Curriculum for Key Stages 3 and 4 (11–16-year-olds), there is no mention of his plays for Key Stages 1 and 2 (5–11-year-olds). The only direct reference is in the History compulsory programme of study on the Tudor period. Hence, primary schools do not generally see Shakespeare as an essential part of their curriculum, although he might appear briefly within the history curriculum; his themes and language are seen as too difficult, too adult, for primary pupils. Also, many teachers lack confidence in approaching Shakespeare, not only because of the assumed pupils' response but because they are uncertain of their own ability to understand and speak it.

There are exceptions, however, and we find examples of primary schools who have introduced Shakespeare to mixed-ability groups either as a classroom activity or through school productions, not necessarily using play-texts in their entirety, but adapted and approached in a way that is appropriate to the experience of the pupils. Many of these examples have been recorded and encouraged by the Shakespeare and Schools Project directed by Rex Gibson at the Institute of Education, Cambridge University.

In seeking to introduce Shakespeare to pupils as young as 5 years, the RSA Project intended to demonstrate that his work can be made accessible and enjoyable to pupils of all ages and abilities, provided the text is chosen carefully and appropriate teaching strategies are used. Teachers avoided reading a whole play with a class from beginning to end; instead they looked within plays for themes that would engage their pupils, and introduced them through methods that encouraged active participation.

> I can now see there are so many possibilities of using Shakespeare in the primary classroom, and I am determined to look for interesting ways of using the plots and the language of his works.
>
> (Teacher, Lady Jane Grey Primary)

Teaching approaches were guided by two principal considerations. First, teachers worked on the premise that they need not use the whole of the text, and that success would be achieved if their pupils became so engaged in the plays that they wanted to find out more without being driven. Secondly, although the initial approach might be through the theme, story or characters, pupils must come into contact with the language and acquire some sense of the meaning of the text, the imagery and the rhythms. These considerations applied right across the age range.

> But for all the children the magic of Shakespeare is in his language, from the 5-year-olds who quickly incorporated Orsino and Sir Toby Belch into their play and the 7-year-old quoting 'By the pricking of my thumbs' to the older pupils who demanded unadulterated Shakespearean speeches.
>
> (Teacher, Kirby Muxloe Primary)

In seeking to involve pupils through active approaches to the plays, teachers were aware that any approach can be as arid or limiting as the driest desk-bound academic approach. No method is infallible, and this becomes all too apparent in some books and articles on Shakespeare, where illustrations depict children acting out Shakespeare without understanding and using empty, meaningless gestures.

The accounts of the work in this volume have been written by primary school teachers for colleagues, who face the same daily pressures and demands of the classroom. In selecting which accounts to include, we have concentrated on those that have approached a Shakespeare play directly, with no intention of discounting work which was sparked off by the Project and which is just as justifiable educationally, such as Martinshaw Primary's production of *The Heir of Caldecote*, a play set in Shakespeare's times. The school had been working on the Tudors as part of the National Curriculum and the teachers decided to aim for what they described as the 'sights and sounds' of the period. The play, which tells the story of David Lucy and his eventual meeting with William Shakespeare, provided a useful framework for looking at life in the Tudor period. The pupils were involved in activities of the period and in the functioning of the court of Queen Elizabeth. The play led the class to the Globe Theatre where the final scene showing Hamlet's death was enacted. *The Heir of Caldecote* was later presented at the Festival. Di Watson, the class teacher, writes of the work:

> The Tudors really came to life on our costume day. This was spent learning about life in Tudor England through miniature painting, sonnet writing, dancing, singing and finally dressing in Tudor costume and visiting the court of Good Queen Bess. 'I'm a boy and no way am I wearing that' became 'now this is how you do History!' As our Hamlet breathed his last the children automatically focused on him. They understood that this was what their Shakespeare journey had all been about, leading them to the man himself. Hopefully their next meeting with him will be just as rewarding.

Newtown Linford village school staged a Tudor event in the village hall in which the whole school, pupils and staff, and many parents were directly involved. The deputy head, David Ashfield, describes the event:

> The Tudor happening? No less than a visit by Good Queen Bess to a village fete, where she is entertained to much music, dancing and eventually a rambling madrigalian ditty that is mercifully interrupted by news of the Spanish Armada sighting. Pausing to rehearse her coming Tilbury speech ('Though I may have the body of a weak and feeble woman, I have the heart ...') Elizabeth sweeps out to fanfares, acclaim and more village celebration. Earlier in the proceedings, she had been invited to view a scene from 'Master Shakespeare's new play' (we gambled on the audience not knowing that Macbeth was probably written in James I's time).
>
> The scene is the witches' meeting with Macbeth and Banquo ('What are these so withered and so wild in their attire?'). The three girls who played the weird women were quite outstanding – the words were Will's but the evil cackles their very own. As they tossed the foul ingredients in the cauldron, the watching ring of infants joined in with gleeful hissing.

The rest of the dialogue was as close to Shakespeare as we could get with a smattering of adapted quotations tricked out with amateur pastiche ...

'Welcome, gracious sovereign, to this place
Well do its citizens admire the face
Thou show'st the scoundrel Spanish in their course
To conquer England, and to give us wars ... '

It was very well received by the audience, happily in the same village hall in which the Keystage players had performed some weeks previously.

The staff had been involved in researching ancient nursery rhymes, children's games, songs and dances. Despite our efforts we could find out little about the steps of a courtly Elizabethan to a recorder tune from Much Ado About Nothing. The flings of the peasant folk were represented by traditional circle dances. Live music was provided by recorders and keyboard/harpsichord playing contemporary pieces; introductory, incidental and concluding music from recordings of groups who recreate authentic sounds on replica instruments. Later we also recorded and watched the play from the BBC Shakespeare Animated Tales series.

The children enjoyed it all; as a whole-school cross-curricular event it was a success. We could put little ticks in boxes to prove what the children learnt from all this – and later a little cross to show they'd remembered it. But who would be enough of a Gradgrind to reduce such an experience so? It was enough that we felt and believed it was worthwhile. Feelings and beliefs still play a necessary part in education.

Elizabeth Woodville Primary involved classes in Years 5 and 6 in work on Shakespeare and the Tudors in the context of a whole term project on 'Our Heritage', as seen from the outline planning diagram. This and other diagrams and children's work are reproduced by kind permission of the schools, parents and the children themselves. Plays on which the programmes were based included *Twelfth Night*, *The Tempest*, *A Midsummer Night's Dream*, *King Lear*, *A Winter's Tale*, *The Merchant of Venice*, *Hamlet* and *Macbeth*.

Chapter 2

Thornton Primary School

A Midsummer Night's Dream as Enjoyed by One Mixed-ability Class of 8–10-year-olds in a Small Village School

Muriel Walker

In Thornton Primary, a village school with just over a hundred pupils, two mixed-ability classes, one for Years 3 and 4 and the other for Years 5 and 6, worked on *A Midsummer Night's Dream*. The class teachers worked initially with drama advisory staff to introduce the play in a practical way through role play. The class of younger pupils, supported by the head teacher, Elise Watchorn, responded to the play through discussion, writing and a wide range of art and craft activities, which resulted in a very lively display in the Shakespeare Exhibition. The older pupils aged 8–10 years and their teacher, Muriel Walker, presented their own twenty-minute adaptation in school and as part of the Shakespeare Festival. All the pupils in the school followed the development of the production. There was a total involvement of the whole school – pupils, staff, parents and governors. *Editor*.

Involvement in the Shakespeare Project represented initially a challenge for me as a teacher. Was it possible to teach some aspect of Shakespeare in a way that made it relevant and meaningful to my mixed-ability class of 8–10-year-olds? I was enthusiastic about the idea, and was soon to find this enthusiasm mirrored in other teachers working on the Project.

So what happened?

I think it is possibly best to let events, and the children, speak for themselves. As our work progressed I recorded, in diary form, the development of our studies of *A Midsummer Night's Dream*.

This extract concerns a visit made to school by Rick Lee, the drama advisory teacher, who had previously met with the children and introduced Puck to them. They knew that the plot involved fairy beings, and that Oberon and Titania were involved in a disagreement; little more.

Rick's welcome came in the form of the familiarity with which the children greeted him:

'Has Puck come?'

'Did you know Shakespeare's been on the tele?'

'Are you going to tell us some more about them two that has fell out?'

He reminded them of the play's title. Silence fell, then Ashley ventured, 'Who's in it?' Philip happily remembered, 'Puck is.' Rick suggested that Puck would be a possible source of information. Having eagerly and successfully effected Rick's transformation into Puck they began to establish him more fully, asking,

'Where do you live?'
'Where I like.'
'Under the sea?'
'I told you, where I like. You don't listen; mortals never listen properly.'

After more of this, they asked him about the 'row'. Puck was annoyingly and deliberately evasive but did reveal other names plus his own comments on the characters:

'You might see Theseus, he's ever so posh, thinks he's important. So does Philostrate, bossing everyone about. Some of the mortals are quite, quite stupid; one's called Bottom!'

Suddenly a casual comment caused Puck to disappear. This only conveyed to the children the mercurial nature of this 'being', encouraged the children to consider how best to use Puck's time, and taught them to eliminate unnecessary questions. Once Puck had flown, Rick gave the children the opportunity to see the cast list. They began immediately to 'investigate' it. Within a short space of time they had identified Athens as 'being Greek', recalled Theseus as 'the Minotaur chap', sorted out 'posh names', decided which were fairies and laughed at the funny-sounding Quince, Snug, Bottom, Flute, Snout and Starveling. One group speculated, 'I bet Flute talks squeakily, and Snout has a nose like a pig, squashed at the end.'

Rick announced that they were now ready to visit Titania's enchanted forest. He conferred this as a great honour and it was accepted as such. Back we went to our classroom to await our visit in an atmosphere like that of the 'robing-room'.

Called back into the hall, we saw that there was some blue material on the floor, and what appeared to be a silver staff.

The children clamoured round Rick as he told them that we were about to re-enact the 'row' between the Fairies and that he would become Titania. There were cries of disbelief.

'You can't! She's a queen.'

Philip was particularly vociferous in his decision to play no part in this! Others began, lured by Philip's popularity, to side with him.

'It's silly.'
'What're you putting on, then? A dress?'
'I ain't being a fairy in a dress.'

None of this worried Rick in the slightest, though I was beginning to feel perturbed! He again talked to them about the power of imagination, how it can be made to work, or left lying idle. He did this patiently and with no urgency. His final remark was, 'It will only work if you can make it.' The dissenters rose to this thinly disguised challenge! Within a minute I was taken aback to hear them telling Rick that I would 'be Oberon'! They then divided themselves into the two camps, becoming either Titania's fairies or Oberon's guards. Ashley elected to be the 'changeling boy', loved by Titania. I was duly presented with my share of the blue material to effect my own transformation. I caught the children's nervousness as they listened for three taps made on the floor by Rick's wielding of his silver wand. At each tap they were to freeze, waiting as Rick donned one piece of material. By the time the third tap had sounded, the forest glade encompassed Titania and her ministering fairies, while, somewhere in the environs, Oberon and minions began their progress towards confrontation. Just for this one moment alone, involvement in the Project was justified! Not a twig moved; not a fairy breathed. Titania imperiously lifted her staff, and Oberon took a deep breath. The changeling boy lay at Titania's feet as she asked for a drink. Her querulous tones told us not to displease her.

There are only seven girls in my class, and all had elected to be in Titania's camp. Among these was one who had been rather frightened by Rick's transformation into Puck. I watched her face, and saw that, as a fairy, she felt quite safe as one of the others flitted to 'fetch a drink'. The girls had sprouted imaginary wings, and could only move by dint of spreading their arms, extending their fingers, and gently wafting the air so that they could glide along. With all the delicacy of a noviciate priest handling a chalice, the fairy (Charlotte) brought Titania her drink. She knelt gracefully and proffered the imaginary cup. Rick took it, quaffed its contents and turned purple with rage, spraying the drink from his offended lips.

Titania:	Ugggh! How dare you? WHAT did I tell you to do?
Fairy:	(*Shielding her head with her wings*) I brought you a drink, your majesty.
Titania:	And WHAT have you brought, dolt?
Fairy:	Wine, it's wine.
Titania:	Are you trying to poison me?
Fairy:	No, I wouldn't do that, your majesty.
Titania:	Then why have you given me human's filthy muck? You should know that fairies cannot eat mortal food. Fetch me a proper drink.

The fairies were horrified, but the changeling boy was seen to smile. The chastened fairy returned with what, she assured Titania, was 'wild strawberry juice'. Titania and the other fairies admired its glowing colour and savoured its bouquet!

But, if they had expected Titania to be appeased, the relief was only temporary because now her nostrils were flaring in anger as she scented the imminent arrival of Oberon. Worse than that, SHE had been the first to smell what she described as the dank, stagnant odour; so what did her look-outs have to say in way of explanation? Why had they sounded no warning? They could offer no excuse that she would accept as reasonable, being, as it was, stunned into silence! Titania was in a fine rage.

Oberon and his solemn, overawed minions were within hailing distance. A fairy was sent as go-between to ask why Oberon had dared to offend Titania by 'invading her space'.

Oberon was no easier to approach than Titania. He wanted, not to indulge in idle chatter, but to take away with him 'the pup that fawns at her feet'.

The changeling boy was visibly offended by being thus described.

Insults began to fly through the air, faithfully transmitted by the fairies.

They did try to temper what each warring party said by altering the tone of voice in which it was spoken!

Regrettably these 'brisk and giddy-paced times' had to end there as the planned time had drawn to a close without our noticing its passing.

The children were reluctant to leave, and this was a true indication of their involvement in, and enjoyment of, what had happened.

The old-fashioned, unfamiliar words that had become interspersed with familiar, modern ones in our 'acting' had not caused a moment's pause.

(Mention must be made of an 'extra' who appeared but briefly. Just as we were being both delighted and alarmed by Titania's vagaries of mood, the hall door opened and in came one of our classroom ancillaries. This kind lady was holding a cup and saucer in her hand and was looking for Mr Lee. Through the semi-gloom and the serried ranks of assorted ethereal beings she made her faltering progress until she approached Titania's throne where Rick sat, swathed in blue bed-linen and bearing aloft his be-foiled branch. In a bright, matter-of-fact voice, she offered, 'Tea?' The answering terse, 'NO thank you!' so surprised her that both Titania AND Oberon were left tea-less!)

Christmas approached and we were heavily committed to rehearsing for our school pantomime. An additional treat was a visit to the Theatre in Education company's production of *Macbeth*. The children were living in such a dramatic whirl that I wondered whether they would be able to disentangle Duncan from the briars round Sleeping Beauty's castle, or Puck from Birnam Wood! We decided to temporarily shelve Shakespeare!

Thus it was that we came back from the holidays 'refreshed' and eager to continue the work. Would it be an easy task to pick up the threads, or would they have become ravelled or even lost by the children?

What luck! Santa brought Joseph a beautiful copy of *Shakespeare's Stories*, written by E. Nesbit and containing *A Midsummer Night's Dream*! On a rainy afternoon, with the children sitting on the carpet, I began to read them the story.

'Hermia and Lysander loved each other, but Hermia's father, Egeus, wanted her to marry Demetrius.'
'Oh, this is the real people in the story,' said Victoria.
'Yes, and we were supposed to be doing that play, and we never did!' added Philip, accusingly.
'Can you remember it?' I asked.
'Yes! Yes! Let's do it now!' they enthused and were shambling to their feet when Sheana stopped us. 'Can't we put this new bit in about the real people?

What do they do?' With a complete swing of mood they all sat down again and someone picked up the book.

The story was slow to unfold as it is so convoluted, and it was interrupted by many questions. I found that I was actually reading the plot of a play to a bunch of aspiring actors who were soon to assume the roles. The questions were all concerned with interpretation.

'Would Hermia be crying or was she mad?'
'Did Egeus choose Demetrius because he was rich?'
'Is Oberon more powerful than Titania?'
'Can Puck do what he likes, or does Oberon boss him around?'
'Why does Helena want Demetrius if he don't like her no more?'

When I judged that enough new information had been given to them, I asked, 'Do you think that you can put that into your play?' Not in the least daunted by the task, they immediately began to make plans. I suggested that they work through each scene in turn, trying to involve everyone in the class. They were spurred on by the realization that they could each take part in most of the scenes, and that different roles would have to be adopted.

'Let's have it all over the place and have everybody sitting around.'
'We can have some weird music that gets you excited.'
'You don't have to tell people who you are ... you just go off in a corner and come back as someone else.'
'We could wear masks on the back of our heads.'
'You don't have to have real things; you just act them there, like trees.'
'Girls can act men.'

Lunch-time arrived and they went from the classrooms still discussing the play, their precious football lying forgotten!

After lunch I was dismissed into a corner of the hall to crash a cymbal for Theseus's court. From my vantage point behind the dining-table, I watched them sort out the whole series of scenes in a very business-like way. For once, the followers were going along with things enthusiastically. The leaders, also for once, were being both diplomatic and encouraging! (It's all right, Jonathon. You can be a tree because they don't have to speak, but you can turn into an elf with us.)

Busily they worked together towards a common end, and I only intervened when they asked me to do so! As the scenes unfolded, I enjoyed myself as much as the children.

The scenes were as follows:

- Cymbals announce the Duke's arrival. 'You gotta bow to dukes and what-sits.'
- Egeus tells Theseus, 'I've chosen this man because he's handsome and rich but she won't marry him. She's a very stupid girl, my lord.' Hermia is dragged home.

'You'd better come on home, missie, and change your mind.'

- Hermia and Lysander plan to elope. 'Guess what? They're making me marry Demetrius.' 'They can't.' 'They can.' 'They can't.' 'They can. It's the law.'
- Hermia reveals all to Helena. 'Hey, guess what? I'm running off because I don't want to marry Demetrius.' 'Can I have him?' 'Yes,' (giggles), 'I don't want him.' 'Good. I'll have him then.' 'See ya!'
- Distorted children become distorted trees. The lights are turned off for effect, and switched on again rapidly when the moonlight is called for. 'Joseph, don't you make a noise with those switches. You're a moon.'
- Elves and fairies revel with gaiety. A tree is uprooted. Oberon and Titania dodge each other. 'Ill met by moonlight, proud Titania!' Lumbering trees encircle the couple. 'Get in a ring, 'cause that's magic.' Suddenly they fell themselves to make a clearing.
- Oberon ruffles his hair 'to make me look really wild'. 'Give me that Indian Prince!' 'No.' 'I'll just do anything as long as you give him to me.' 'Well, I want a new palace and more fairies.' 'Give him to me!' 'NO! I just love him!' 'Well you said you loved me, once.'
- Titania flies away and Puck zooms in on what sounds like an aerial motor-bike. 'Stop it, Puck!' 'Hey, guess what? I can jump as high as the highest tree in the wood!' 'I'll jump on you, if you don't shut up!'
- Puck goes off to fetch Love-in-Idleness.
- Elves speculate about the effect of the juice. 'What if she sees a slug?' 'Serve her right!' Convulsive laughter runs riot. Titania drifts across to her bank. The ministering fairies fly so close they nearly suffocate her. At last they retreat into a soporific silence.
- Helena trails after Demetrius. 'Hermia's running away. She doesn't want you so I can have you back.' 'I don't want you back.' 'Why not? You used to be my sweetheart.' 'Well, I'm not now. You make me sick to look at you.'

'I wish I hadn't told you, now.'

- Puck returns. Oberon orders him to, 'Find that man from Athens and give him the treatment.' 'Where is he?' 'You know everything, so go and find him.'
- Lysander wanders with Hermia. 'Let's go to sleep. I'm tired but you can sleep over there.' 'You'll be safer if I stay on this bank!' 'No! Go over there.'
- Puck sneaks in. He has obviously abandoned his motorbike in the interests of secrecy. Lysander stirs as the drops touch his eyes. Puck zooms off to a corner and curls up.
- Helena giggles her way through the wood. Lysander awakes. 'Oh, it's Helena! Isn't she beautiful? I don't want Hermia! Helena! Helena!' Arms stretched invitingly wide, he bounds towards Helena. 'Stop it Lysander! You're only mucking me about. That's cruel.'

Though I can capture in words a few of their improvised lines, what I cannot capture here is the wonderful spontaneity that bore them along and the way in which they enjoyed 'playing' together.

'Can we do it for real people?' they asked. Given an affirmative answer they began when time permitted to plan and rehearse their performance.

I watched them rehearse and saw them gradually drawing in all the things they had learned about the play and then adding their own perspectives.

'Craig's a bit quiet when he brings Sile in.'
(Craig and Sile are playing Egeus and Hermia.)
'Well, I don't like shouting.'
'You can be mad and quiet. My Dad can, anyway.'
'You'd be quiet if you were upset, and he's bothered about Hermia.'
'I won't listen if he shouts, anyway.'

'Will they know us if we're fairies AND trees?'
'If you act 'em good they will.'

'I keep forgetting what I'm arguing about.'
'Just keep on at me about the Indian prince and I'll keep persuading you.'

'Puck, you're making me dizzy.'
'I'm doing it to annoy you!'
'Well, it gets on my nerves.'
'Precisely!'

'Turn your foot in; it looks like a tree stump, not a fairy's foot.'
'This'd be dead good in a wood!'
'Yeah! At midnight!'

'Can we have dresses for the court?'
'Oh, shut up! We ain't got time for dresses. Mime 'em.'

When this particular session ended, and the children went out of the hall, eight-year-old Sile said, 'I'm really, really happy!'

The class wanted to tackle the challenge to complete the play as soon as possible.

'Let's just get on and do it all. We can leave everything else.' Told by me that this was not possible, they began to negotiate terms! 'You read it to us, Mrs Walker, and we'll do all the rest and you can watch.' 'It'll be good and it'll be Shakespeare so it's good for schooling and that!'

We all happily agreed with Lewis's suggestion that we, 'Do it every now and then, when it's raining or when we've just had a spelling test or when you're pleased with us or ...' (The list went on.)

That is how we made progress, by picking up and reading or discussing little pieces of the story that they were finding fascinating. I now found that I could read the play 'straight' to them without translating into modern English. They had favourite scenes and favourite phrases that I heard them frequently repeating. (Dismissal at home-time, 'Pray men, we are haunted! Flee!' *Sotto voce*, when chastised by the Road Safety Lady, 'Ill met by moonlight, proud Titania!'

I was using my school-days' copy of the play which they borrowed to browse through and into school I brought all copies of Shakespeare's plays that I could find. They greeted these arrivals with interest, in idle moments looked at cast lists, and found unusual words. If these were all my books, why had I not acted in any of these plays at school? What was the point of just reading them?

Ashley:	Schools should let you act 'em though. You learn more.
Charlotte:	Did you like the words? I love the words.
Lewis:	Yes, the words are alright, but you've got to say 'em.
Sheana:	Acting's the best, and words are second.
Craig:	No, Shakespeare's words are for saying and acting. That's why he wrote them.

So now we know!

It seemed that the stone had landed well and truly in the middle of the pond and the ripples began in earnest. 'We went to a pub called "The Shakespeare".' 'My Gran says he's a bard. What's a bard?' Creative writing and poetry appeared unannounced to be welcomed.

Moth's Story

My name's Moth. My mistress is a queen and I am one of her faithful servants. The others are called Cobweb, Mustard-seed and Peaseblossom ... oh there are many more. My mistress is quite nice but sometimes she can be very nasty. At night we sleep on beds of flowers but my mistress always has the nicest bed. We eat rose petals, wild cherries, apricots and honey from bees' nests. We have to collect butterfly wings to fan our mistress with. All the fairies love her really. If she found out that I talk to mortals she would NOT be pleased.

One sunny morning we woke up to hear her stamping around. She was muttering, '"Ill-met by moonlight" indeed! We'll see about that!' We thought that she had obviously been to see Oberon and they'd had another of the rows they seem to enjoy! We tried to calm her down but she would not be calmed down. She said that she was tired of Oberon accusing her of causing trouble and that, of course, it was all his fault. The real truth of the trouble is the Indian Prince. He is what is causing Oberon's jealousy. Titania thinks she loves the Indian Prince; Oberon says she is pampering him like a puppy. We fairies all love the Indian boy, and that is what Oberon can't stand; he is used to us all loving him!

We had just sung the queen to sleep, and it took a long time, I can tell you, when stomping through the bushes came a silly ass-like man. What happened? TITANIA WOKE UP AND FELL IN LOVE WITH HIM! We think there is something seriously wrong with Titania. We have to look after this creature as though he is something beautiful and special. He's really ugly. I don't know what Titania can be thinking of. Something very odd is happening.

I don't know how it will all end.

(Victoria Lee)

Plans for an ideal setting were drawn showing caves and hideouts within the wood, with Acropolis-type drawings of Theseus's Court kept well to the edge. Many of the drawings showed circles where the fairies were to meet, which echoed their groupings when acting the play. I asked whether they could group all the characters into circles. They found this an easy task and we soon had four circles: courtiers, mechanicals, fairies and lovers.

I asked, 'Is there any character that could be in two circles?'
Answers came swiftly.

'Puck. He's a fairy and he mucks about with the mechanicals.'
'Hermia. She's in the court and in the lovers' ring.'
'All the fairies go in the court at the end.'
'And the mechanicals go to the court.'
'Bottom can go in three circles, the mechanicals, 'cause he is one, the court, 'cause he goes there and the fairies 'cause Titania gets him.'
'Why do some characters go from group to group?' I asked.
'That's how the play joins all the bits together,' answered Ashley.

They then had great fun linking characters to each other. The children drew interlocking circles and positioned the characters accordingly. We also played a game with a ball of string. Everyone sat in a circle with the ball of string, the idea being that one character passes the ball on to another character with whom he/she can prove a connection in the play. The criss-crossing string serves as an aid to show how many links there are. The children loved doing this and found so many possible links that the ball nearly completely unwound!

Whenever we had a few spare minutes, we went into the hall to carry on with 'rehearsals'. I left the planning to them. When they needed help, they asked me for it, but I felt that it was very important for them to see this presentation as their own creation. The problems that presented themselves usually occurred when all the children had to move around at the same time, or when there was a large number of unoccupied children. (Aren't these the common problems of the classroom?) I suggested that they could use people to make Quince's house, and that moving about as fairies or courtiers *en masse* would become easier if they thought in patterns. They accepted these suggestions with alacrity, decided to build Quince's house with three 'walls', to enter two-by-two as courtiers, and to move the fairies round in flying circles. They tried out all these manoeuvres with a great deal of squabbling until order was established.

'LOOK!' demands Oberon, 'You've gotta get up off the floor and run round in a ring till me and Titania say you can go.'
'Yes, but I keep getting pushed out,' complains an elf.
'There's too much pushing,' criticizes Titania, 'You look like footballers, not fairies.'
'I'm not flying round like a butterfly, like you,' asserts another elf.
'Well, we've got to be in a circle so you've got to run properly,' insists Her Fairy Majesty.

'Yes,' Oberon says, 'Get up in turn, starting at the back and run behind me and Titania and NO OVERTAKING!'

'Don't thump about, then, or it spoils it,' adds Cobweb.

'And don't go too fast or we'll bump into each other when Oberon stops,' advises a tree.

I wonder whether this is my class, or whether I have been magically transported to the wood to watch the mechanicals!

They try the running circle and Puck (inevitably) skids and fells two trees, a fairy and the Duke of Athens. They all roll about laughing, pick themselves up, try again with more decorum and succeed in making an orderly exit.

The play began (literally!) to fall into shape. Quite often I was asked to read a certain scene again to make it 'right' for them.

Acting the play became the highlight of their days. It became just as common to find a group of children sitting on the playground wall discussing whether Oberon would ever get the better of Titania, as it was to find a group swapping football cards!

Eventually, and all in the space of a few weeks, the play was ready to perform. We invited parents and friends into school to see the play and needed to have two performances, such was the response. We performed to the whole school and laughed delightedly to see a 4-year-old running across the playground, arms outstretched, calling, 'Helena! Helena!' performing his version of Lysander after he had seen the play.

The early years' classes drew pictures for us, and we were amazed by the way in which their drawings reflected the patterns within the play, particularly the fairy circles that the players had tried so hard to perfect. We had a visit from Mr Andrew Fairbairn, the Chairman of the RSA Arts Advisory Group, and performed for him and his fellow visitors, all squashed into our classroom and leaping over recumbent bodies!

Then came the evening when we went to Groby Community College to perform part of the celebration of the Project. Oh, the thrill of waiting in the wings! Oh, the pleasure of hearing the audience laugh! The children's faces actually glowed with delight. They were successful, and they knew it! So enthusiastic was the young lad's performance that the Shakespeare Project Chairman, Philip Watson, was moved to announce in his closing remarks, 'When I grow up, I want to be a Wall!'

I knew then what involvement in the Shakespeare Project had accomplished for us all. Our approach had been positive from the outset, teachers and children had worked together towards a common end. There had been time to talk about what we hoped for and to discuss what we had achieved. Each child's contribution had been valued by the others. Our expectations had been high, and the children had been kept in the permanent mood of expecting success. This in itself brought causes, events and opportunities, which brought success.

We were invited to take our performance to Kirby Muxloe Primary School and to South Charnwood High School and these visits we gladly undertook. Our 'team' feels that it can tackle anything nowadays!

Whenever, in the future, these children hear the name 'Shakespeare', it will instantly recall a time of great enjoyment.

Maple leaves falling

Autumn winds gusting high
                    in the trees

Growing plants struggling .

In this forest is enchantment,
                              the

Call of my sweet bird friends.

Are these the fairies

Lying sleeping? Or dead leaves?

                    Alex Myers.
                    (Aged 8)

Mangold   THORNTON CP   Edprint, Telford (0952) 48623

Figure 2.1

Lysander's Story

Well I suppose it all started like this. I was in the forest with Hermia and she told me that she could not marry me because she had to marry Demetrius,. This was what her Father said, so she had to. We didn't do the thing she was told to do....we made a plan. She would meet me in the forest at dusk that very night. She came to meet me with her cheeky smile and a glint in her eyes. She said, "Where are we going to, Lysander?" I said "We'll go to my Aunt's place." "What good will that do?" she asked. "Well, she's got a place outside Athens, and the law's different there."
"How far is it to your Aunt's place?" "Not far," I said, stroking her lovely long hair, "but I'm tired." Hermia agreed that she was too and we lay down on a grassy bank. I offered to keep Hermia safe and warm, but she made me lie on another bank and we went to sleep. When I woke up I saw Helena and I loved her with all my love. I forgot about Hermia. Helena looked so beautiful...I ran after her through the trees.

Jamie Hincks.   THORNTON CP

Figure 2.2

My master the King of the Wood, fell out with Titania, the Queen of the Wood. Oberon ordered me to get a flower called "Love-in Idleness". While I had gone to fetch it, Oberon told the other elves what the flower would do. It had the power to put love into your eyes, so that whoever you saw first you'd love.

There were lovers in the wood called Helena, Hermia, Lysander and Demetrius. My master Oberon saw Demetrius insult Helena and he wanted to help her. So, when I got back, he told me to put the magic juice in Demetrius's eyes so that he would love Helena again and that would solve their quarrel. He meant well.

I put the juice in Lysander's eyes by mistake. It was an easy mistake to make as they were both dressed in clothes like they wore in Athens, and they were both wandering round in the woods. I don't usually make mistakes. If I do something wrong I usually do it on purpose.

There were some other people wandering around in the wood practising a play for the Duke of Athens. I jumped out and put an ass's head on one of them and all the others ran away.

The Wood is my place.

Alex Myers.   Puck's Story.

THORNTON   March '93

Figure 2.3

Participation in the Project began at a time when morale in the teaching profession seemed to have reached an all-time low. Any effort ceases to be re-creative the moment it becomes wearisome. We all need new challenges if we are not to stagnate. Knowingly, I intended to give the children creative opportunities; unknowingly, I was to give myself a reminder of all the reasons which prompted me to become a teacher. I feel that I was privileged to share in something very special.

Finally, let one of my pupils have the last word.

'What're we doing next, Miss? There's a lot to go at.'

Chapter 3

Coleman Junior School

A *Midsummer Night's Dream* in a Multi-cultural Context

Ed Farrow

Coleman Primary, an inner-city school with over 600 pupils, has a high proportion of minority groups. For many of the pupils, English is a second language. In contrast to Thornton Primary, the school decided from the outset to undertake a formal production of scenes from A *Midsummer Night's Dream* that would be presented in school and at the Shakespeare Festival. A group of pupils were selected to do the mechanicals' scenes which were augmented by a programme of music presented by a choir and orchestra. *Editor.*

'Of course, as you may know, our school has a strong commitment to the Leicestershire Shakespeare Project which we would like to continue if possible. Are you familiar with the aims?'

I was having a chat with the head of the school to which I had recently been appointed. Common sense dictated that I should take the bull by the horns and admit complete ignorance and a certain amount of alarm. I should have been open and frank, earning respect for honesty and integrity ... 'Oh yes,' I said.

Visited that night by pangs of guilt and visions of horror that closely rivalled Richard III before Bosworth, I determined to find out what the nature of this beast might be. Having further learned that the substance of our school's contribution had not been determined, I began the great search for evidence as to what the Shakespeare Project might be. Excavating in the cupboard I soon found what I was seeking. A booklet describing the nature of the project and the schools involved was extracted from a pile of language documents. Wiping away the thin film of grey dust so peculiar to schools I sat down to learn my fate.

My predecessor had determined to make a contribution from A *Midsummer Night's Dream* focusing on courts and processions. Ah! I knew *The Dream* but alas my knowledge of courts and processions was not all it should be. At the back of my mind was the thought that I had a full Christmas production to cast and direct so that my drama workload during the next couple of months would be full to say the least. Some kind of contribution of students' work was to be required by some time in March at a Shakespeare Festival ... I reburied the information carefully for re-excavation the following spring!

Not having any formal training in drama I came to its pleasures late in life. Although using drama had always been a feature of my classroom practice, my greatest pride came from cobbling together productions for school consumption. How quickly Christmas came and went and the dawning of that dreaded day when Shakespeare could be put off no longer. I already knew that I wanted our contribution to be some drama performance rather than another related area of the curriculum. But which play and which bit?

The head stepped in with the suggestion of the mechanicals' play from *A Midsummer Night's Dream*, which of course I rejected out of hand on the grounds that head teachers are rarely right in any matters of great weight. It did, however, prompt me to look again – and, yes, reluctantly, it might be a workable idea. Some ideas began to form.

Reading the text, of course, brought back many happy memories of productions seen in the past. Even though the text was familiar I was often scurrying to the back of the book to look at those microscopic footnotes. How on earth were my children going to cope with this? I was sure I was going to have to translate the text into something approaching twentieth-century speech to make the play at all accessible.

Many days later I sat with pen poised ready to perform the update. The mechanicals actually have three scenes:

1. Casting their play
2. The rehearsal in the wood
3. The performance before the Duke of Athens

The speeches range through prose, blank verse and formal verse.

Many days later I had learned these simple truths one by one:

1. You can't translate any part of the verse without altering the meaning, or resorting to writing your own personal doggerel, which you might be proud of in ordinary circumstances, but not with Shakespeare in front of you.
2. The prose is difficult to translate as it still contains references and concepts outside the range of primary children's experience.
3. Some parts can be cut, especially obscure references that didn't affect the body of meaning.

So there I was, left with a very untranslated script for those three short scenes, wondering what my Year 5 and Year 6 customers would think of it.

Our school is one of the largest primaries in Leicester with a very large majority of the children from ethnic minority backgrounds. Muslims, Sikhs and Hindus are almost equally represented.

I approached casting with some anxiety because I was unsure of the response of children to this 'alien' kind of English, especially those children whose first language was not English at all. At least I had some indications of their drama capabilities from the previous production. Hearing the words of Shakespeare come from such young mouths was at first a strange experience. They seemed to read it with some enjoyment. Initial feelings of pleasure were somewhat dulled when I began to realize that although they were decoding it well, even simple questions about what they had read produced raised eyebrows and shoulders. We sat down and we talked ... then we talked some more ... and more. While we read I became aware that they were beginning to look on the text as some kind of secret code that they were determined to crack. They were initially attracted by the sound and rhythm of the words and later by the funny words that they hadn't heard before. Their interest increased as they began to comprehend and the meaning became clear.

There was a worry; we were three weeks into rehearsal and hadn't moved a single passage or scene. They became fascinated by the tortuous plot, they began to pick out the peculiarities of the characters. They began to explain for themselves some of the verbal jokes, yet still there was no moving the piece.

Explanations began to take on a Byzantine complexity. For example, when Bottom says 'a lover is more pathetic' the process went as follows:

> 'I'll find "pathetic" in the dictionary.'
> 'Has Bottom said the wrong word?'
> 'Does he mean sympathetic?'

There is a scuffling to find those minuscule footnotes.

> 'Has "pathetic" changed its meaning?'

They were absorbed by the detective work. Their persistence and ingenuity and discoveries even surprised me, when I was confident that I already knew the meaning of a particular line.

The humour of the situation where the children discovered that Shakespeare was using 'rude' words like 'bloody' even when he was 'very famous' helped to lighten the more scholarly episodes.

Those weeks spent talking over the script were worth every minute. When the words became overlaid with the ridiculous action, the slapstick, the visual comedy, they began to laugh out loud and approach the scenes with relish. They overcame something that I had secretly dreaded, that they would lose interest because of the initial difficulties and they would not want to bring it up to performance standards. These were unfounded worries as they always rushed to rehearsal and left wanting to do more.

Any problems? ... Well ... It was some time later that this cosy progress came to an abrupt end. It became obvious that the three scenes were too long so we decided to cut the middle scene and use a short narration instead. My Bottom (Shakespeare's pun) arrived at a rehearsal with a very sore arm and announced he was off to India for a few weeks, but it would be alright wouldn't it because he'd be back just before the first performance? Fighting that nausea which sometimes overwhelms the sensitive director, and after another night with Richard III, we eventually found a creditable replacement.

To make a more rounded production the choir and recorder group had been rehearsed in two contemporary songs – *Under the Greenwood Tree* and *Where the Bee Sucks*. Then came the great day to join forces and stage the whole production. If you have ever thought that actors were a temperamental breed you should try working with musicians. Staging became difficult when the requirements of sound insisted on having that arc of singers and players that make a production so visually wooden. We resolved it by bringing them in as a crowd of spectators and forming them into casual groups. This involved producing one of those floor plans that looks like a kitten's ball of wool.

Another hurdle presented itself on the week of the performance at the Shakespeare Festival. There was a sudden realization that this was the middle of Ramadan.

Our Muslim children, who were performing by kind permission of parents anyway, would have to go on to the stage for the evening performance, not having eaten anything that day. During the few minutes between sunset and the opening of the festival a good many of the cast were force fed with sandwiches!

Apart from major hiccups the production was peppered with the usual mishaps such as the first dress rehearsal when Bottom performed his elaborate dying scene with a rustic tunic determined to ride up to his armpits and expose his day-glo underpants or a performance when Flute disguised as Thisbe forgot her blood-stained mantle – and the missing article was brilliantly mimed by the company. Then there was the time when a member of the choir's supposedly discreet white T-shirt sported the slogan, 'MY DAD'S A BIKER' which was hastily removed and substituted with one worn by the lovely Thisbe. Too late we realized that this garment was the only thing keeping her sponge ball bosom in position.

The whole process of the Shakespeare project was evaluated by an outside agency. When the time came for the students to be interviewed on their thoughts and feelings I was prepared for the worst. Conscious of being deeply immersed in rehearsals, had I provided them with sufficient background? Had we been adventurous enough with our presentation? But most of all what on earth would they say? In the event we were surprised by two things; their knowledge of Shakespeare as an historical personage, and as a prolific writer of other plays. What they most wanted to talk about was how he must have been a very funny comedian on account of his funny plays.

Since the watch word of the project had been to enjoy the Shakespearean experience, the laughter and fun generated by the production more than fulfilled this criterion. Try it and see for yourself!

Chapter 4

Lady Jane Grey Primary School

Bringing Shakespeare to Life through *The Tempest*

Victoria Higgins

Lady Jane Grey Primary looked at ways in which pupils can be introduced to Shakespeare through the characters and dramatic situations in *The Tempest*. The intention was to use Shakespeare as a resource for developing pupils' thinking, communication skills and understanding of relationships and as a stimulus for work in English and art. The class of year 5 and 6 pupils were not presented with any text until they became involved in the story. The teacher first sought to help the children understand the plot and the main themes by bringing to life the main characters. *Editor*.

AN INTRODUCTION

Lady Jane Grey Primary School was asked in June 1992 if we would like to take part in a project to use Shakespeare in the classroom. The staff were sceptical about the inclusion of yet another topic in our already overcrowded curriculum. I was also sceptical about how the class would cope with something that I had found intimidating at school. However, I volunteered my class of Year 5 and 6 children, aged between 9 and 11 years, to take part, hoping that it would develop their confidence in drama, a subject which I found difficult to teach.

Over a series of lessons in which Rick Lee, the advisory teacher for drama, played a number of roles, the children were able to 'call upon' Prospero, Caliban and Ariel: all characters from *The Tempest*. The most exciting part for me was to watch as the children were mystified, annoyed, excited, confused and enthralled by the answers to a variety of questions asked by them of the strange magical visitors. One child said the project was good because it meant 'imagining'. The enjoyment was evident in the way that the children looked forward to the next instalment. Comments were made about Shakespeare being interesting and not just for adults but for everyone. We had many discussions on whether it was Prospero or Caliban who was evil. It was a brilliant way of getting the children interested in the play.

THE BEGINNING

The topic our class had decided to cover in the whole of the Autumn term was 'Explorers and Encounters'. The Shakespeare play that immediately sprang to mind to fit in with this was *The Tempest*. As part of our topic, which included map-making, historical journeys and sea-faring tales, the activity which most caught the minds of the children was the large papier mache island which we built as part of a technology topic.

This island was the focus for our first Shakespeare session. The children were asked to imagine what sounds they would hear on this island. We made a musical map and a tape recording of these noises. These introduced us to the idea that the island was mysterious, and perhaps even magical.

THE ELVES

In our next session, we were privileged to meet Shakespeare himself.

'Who lives on our island?' was the question we addressed next. The class was split into small groups who were each given two lines of a Prospero soliloquy. The children were asked to find out what this speech meant. In order to help them, Shakespeare settled himself down at his desk, ready to answer questions. The children asked very specific questions such as 'What's Ebbing Neptune?' or 'Who's Jove?'

The session was very confusing with children running across the area with excitement.

'He says Neptune is to do with the sea.'
'I've got his autograph!' were some of the comments.

At the end of the session, the children came back together to explain to each other their parts of the speech. The conclusions they came to were: elves were mischievous, they lived on the island, and someone was controlling them. The question was then raised, 'Who controls these elves and all this magic?'

The class went back into their groups, and each group was given one letter. By going around and collecting all the letters, the groups were asked to sort them into a name. (This process was hindered by some mischievous elves giving out the wrong letters.) PROSPERO was the name the class finally came up with. Rick advised us, 'Don't shout his name. He is very powerful.' The class were enchanted with all this magic and mystery. To add to this effect, the next day, when the children came back into the area, a mysterious message had been left by one of the elves, Ariel. It appeared to be a way of calling Prospero. To follow up the session, we made pictures and clay models of our elves, and the children decided they would like to learn their lines.

MEETING PROSPERO

The next session was quite extraordinary. Without any prompting, the children gathered themselves in the hall and organized themselves into a circle. They began to discuss ways of 'calling up' Prospero. In turn, each group formed a smaller circle inside the larger one and began to recite their part of the speech. The class held hands and whispered 'Prospero'.

Suddenly, Rick Lee 'became' the Ariel character. The class, unfamiliar with this way of working, were completely taken aback. Ariel grew cross that the children were not taking Prospero seriously, so he told them if they did not calm down Prospero would not appear. Intrigued by this, the children lay on their backs whispering 'Prospero'. Magically Prospero (Rick sitting cross-legged in the circle) appeared. One at a time and cautiously the confident children began asking questions.

'What kind of clothes do you wear?'
'Do you have any family?'
'Do you fight?'
'Do you live in houses?'

Then the enigmatic answers began to excite the children.

Q: Where do you live?
A: I live in my mind.

Q: Is Ariel more important than Miranda?
A: Miranda in my heart and Ariel in my mind.

Q: What is precious to you?
A: My books.

Q: What is Ariel?
A: Ariel is a free spirit.

After a long and intense session, Prospero agreed to appear again if the children asked more important questions. After Prospero had left, we as a class wrote down all we knew about Prospero. We looked at the Dramatis Personae, to see if we could find out any more. By doing this, we compiled a list of 25 important questions.

WHO IS CALIBAN?

At the next session we began again by 'calling up' Prospero. In the research for our questions, the class became interested in two questions – why was Prospero usurped as a Duke and who is Caliban?

Prospero responded to the questions in a mysterious and elusive way. The children, unhappy with his answers, decided to call next upon Ariel.

Rick suggested that a 'Magical Grove' might entice Ariel to appear. The children obligingly made themselves into twisted and gnarled trees and bushes. They closed their eyes as Ariel did not want to be seen. Ariel (Rick, pouncing on one tree after another) seemed rather a nasty spirit, poking people if they asked awkward questions.

'Are you a sea dryad or a land dryad?' asked one person.

Ariel hissed back that they should mind their own business. Ariel implied in its answers that Prospero was keeping it against its wishes. The children were determined to find out whether Prospero was a 'goody' or a 'baddy'. At this point, Caliban (Rick – a hunched-up figure in the corner of the room) appeared to the children as a weeping, pathetic figure.

A group of children reported to the class that Caliban had had his island taken from him, that it was Prospero who constantly tormented him and had stolen his property. The children were outraged by this injustice and became determined to state Caliban's case to Prospero. However, this proved difficult as it was the end of term and our drama lessons with Rick were temporarily drawing to a close. To be ready for Prospero, some of the children decided they needed to find out the story of *The Tempest*. At silent reading times, I was surrounded by people with not just that particular text, but also many other Shakespeare plays.

Not only had my children been introduced to Shakespeare's works in the drama sessions, they had also enjoyed a visiting theatre group's presentation of *Macbeth*. There were many complimentary comments made by the class, especially about the exciting storylines.

PREPARING FOR THE PERFORMANCE

Unfortunately, due to lack of time, the children were unable to confront Rick in the form of Prospero. However, when he did join us again, he introduced the idea that we may be able to show our work in a real theatre.

A long piece of paper was rolled out along the floor, and the children were asked to split our fifteen minutes of performance time into sections. They then had to decide which section as a small group they would like to direct. The sessions were divided into:

Beginning
Prospero 1
Ariel
Caliban
Prospero 2
End

The class went away to draw up story boards. They were asked to consider ways to capture the audience's imagination and to think about every little detail of how their scene would look. For example, the audience would not be able to see their faces very closely, but would always be able to see the shape of their whole body. We were also advised that it is sometimes more effective if lots of people are doing the same thing rather than each performing individually, and to make this work all 26 of them would have to be concentrating the whole time.

Many children found this planning difficult, as they did not realize just how long three minutes actually were and just how hard it could be getting 26 people to do as they were told. When they began to direct their sections, most groups decided to repeat the meetings with the characters, but difficulties arose for the Prospero 2 group, who had to write for themselves the confrontation between the children and Prospero.

The beginning and ending groups had to make up something new and exciting to link the other pieces. Rick and I tried to encourage them to use a storm to fit in with the play, but the children had their own ideas. Unfortunately, they included drums and flashing lights which they slowly realized were not as effective as they expected. Also, the children wanted to add jokes and to finish with a modern song, but we persuaded them that it would spoil the atmosphere which the rest of the performance had generated. The beginning and ending groups needed more teacher input than the others but were still pleased with their own direction.

As a teacher, I was concerned with several different issues. First of all, would the audience understand the process we had gone through to get to this stage? Secondly, as a child-centred performance, would our school be of the same standard as the other groups? Thirdly, I could not foresee how anyone would be able to take on role as well as Rick. Could the children get into the role of such complex characters? Finally, would any of this be ready in time, as it seemed to be taking so long for the children to decide what was going to happen?

WRITING THE SCRIPT

Writing the script for the performance was the one activity where only a part of the class could join in. All of the children had a feeling about the kind of answers Prospero would give, but it was only a few who could use the text and their imagination to write in Elizabethan speech.

A group of children decided to use the text of *The Tempest* to get the feel of Shakespeare's language. They looked at many of Prospero's speeches to try to work out the answers to some of the questions. Some children thought that Prospero had killed Caliban's mother, so we looked to see whether we could find the truth in the book.

It was through exploring the text that the children began to see Prospero in a better light. Caliban became the one seen as aggressive and unpleasant. This changed the feel of the performance.

Some children were able to extract quotations and use them in the right context in their section of the play. Other children were able to use ideas found in the text and change these into their own words, while still keeping the flavour of the original language.

With the script written, we came even closer to a finished piece of work.

THE PERFORMANCE

Our production was based around a huge piece of red silky material which the children used initially as Prospero's cape. We needed to be taught how to manage it and it proved to be a wonderful way of keeping the class occupied when some of the children's interest might otherwise have waned!

We decided that the performance should reflect the work we had done in the classroom. The opening section included sounds made with voices only, very like the work we had done in the first drama session. The children wanted to make a big impact on the audience, so they entered the stage with a gradually increasing moaning sound, and the large red cloth was unfurled. They sat in a horseshoe shape and whispered 'Prospero'. Prospero slowly emerged from beneath the cloth. Several children asked him questions, based on those from the first meeting with Rick as Prospero. This time the pupil playing Prospero answered in the same elusive and mysterious way.

The children playing the main roles had watched Rick carefully over the weeks and were able to use this experience to portray these complex characters. Most notably the two children playing Prospero, using a fixed stare, were each in turn able to portray the role of a learned and powerful magician.

The children formed their twisted tree shapes and turned the stage into the Magical Grove. A young Ariel flitted and danced her way around, answering the questions put to her. We used voices again to bring the forest to life, and also to solve the problem of knowing where Ariel should go to answer each question. The person about to speak next made a howling sound, so that Ariel had time to get to them ready to provide her answer.

Three children became the deformed monster Caliban. The rest of the group changed into mischievous elves, poking and annoying Caliban. The three children linked arms and huddled together to form one creature. Each elf, before asking the question, prodded Caliban who opened up and with one voice shouted an aggressive response.

After answering several questions, Caliban was asked what he would like to do to Prospero. Everyone sat very still as a 'think-bubble' appeared over Caliban's head, and one of the children read out what appeared there. It was a condensed speech from the text, the gist of which, the children had decided, was that Caliban wanted to kill the Magician.

The red cloth appeared again and the class turned back into their horseshoe shape for Prospero to appear once more.

'What happened to Caliban's mother?'
'She was mortal,' was his echoing reply.

For the end of the performance, the children left the stage in a spiral to the sound of howling voices, leaving one last performer holding a scroll. Again, using part of the original text, she informed us that now Prospero was free of the accusations against him he could burn his books and leave the island.

CONCLUSION

The whole project was, in my view, an outstanding success; it wasn't just the children's excellent performance in the Festival that swayed my opinion, it was the way that everything came together.

I was delighted that our performance reflected the work that had initially been intended only for the classroom. Everything we had done in the drama sessions had been condensed into a fifteen-minute performance. Thus it was able to be mostly the children's work and ideas in keeping with our school ethos. Another successful coming-together was the way we had worked as a group. All the class had taken part; the shyer, more nervous children had been well supported by others with more confidence. Everyone had worked together both in the drama sessions and when directing the production. We really benefited from the shared experience of the performance itself as we all shared our nerves beforehand and the elation afterwards.

Another benefit of the project has been the children's confidence with drama. They are keen to develop their own plays, which are now more mature and interesting. They now insist on making their own props and waiting in 'The Green Room'! The display of work from all the schools at the Festival was wonderful for the children to see, and for me as a teacher it worked as another source of inspiration to introduce Shakespeare into the classroom. It was another source of pride for the children where again they had raised the quality of their work for the occasion.

Being slightly cynical, I wondered how long the interest in Shakespeare would last, and how long-lasting these new skills and the increase in confidence would be. Several weeks after the end of the project, someone brought into school 'The Animated Tales' video of *The Tempest* as seen on television. The children watched in silence and when it was over they burst spontaneously into a heated discussion.

'Prospero was really powerful, wasn't he?'
'Caliban wasn't such a monster.'
'Is it right that someone should take someone else's home?'

I was amazed to hear such young people talking so excitedly about the plot and the characters of a play written over four hundred years ago.

I still feel it is highly inappropriate to expect children of primary age to read through the text 'cold' to get to know the story. Nor can I ever see myself being talented enough to switch into a Shakespearean role in the way that an experienced drama teacher can. However, I can now see there are so many possibilities for using Shakespeare in the primary classroom, and I am determined to look for interesting ways of using the plots and language of his works.

EXTRACTS FROM THE SCRIPT EVOLVED BY LADY JANE GREY PRIMARY SCHOOL FROM THE EXPLORATION OF THE TEMPEST

PROSPERO 1

Child: How does it feel to have a brother who cheats to be a Duke when you yourself should be one?

Prospero: It troubles me, but not much as long as I am the Duke of my own mind.

Child: How many elves work for you?

Prospero: As many as there are pebbles on the beach, leaves on the trees and drops in the rain.

Child: Why do you single Ariel out?

Prospero: Ariel my brave spirit, who is so fair and so constant, who does not affect my reason.

Child: Why have you so many names?

Prospero: Because I am so many people.

Child: Who is the most important person in your life?

Prospero: Miranda in my heart, Ariel in my mind.

Child: Do you protect your daughter from Caliban?

Prospero: I protect her from many things.

Child: Has Caliban met your daughter when you were not there?

Prospero: I pray not.

Child: Do you know who stole the island from Caliban?

Prospero: Not I. Who knows?

ARIEL

Tree: Is Prospero a part of you?

Ariel: I am not of his kind. I am a spirit, a free spirit.

Tree: What do you look like?

Ariel: Mind your own business.

Tree:	Why did Prospero lie to you?
Ariel:	He said he would let me go but he hasn't.

Tree:	Do you like Miranda?
Ariel:	She is beautiful ... for a human.

Tree:	Do you like Caliban?
Ariel:	He is a poor misshapen animal who understands little.

Tree:	What did Prospero do to Caliban?
Ariel:	That I do not know.

Tree:	Do you understand Caliban?
Ariel:	When he is in a good mood I understand but when he is in a bad mood he speaks a language I cannot understand.

Tree:	Why did Prospero imprison Caliban?
Ariel:	That I cannot answer.

CALIBAN

Elf:	Did your parents have magic?
Caliban:	NO.

Elf:	Have you always lived on this island? YES.

Elf:	When did your mother die?
Caliban:	Don't know.

Elf:	Do you like Ariel?
Caliban:	Alright.

Elf:	How does it feel to be a monster?
Caliban:	NOT A MONSTER!

Elf:	Oh yes you are.
Caliban:	NOT.

Elf:	Do you think Prospero's mad?
Caliban:	Prospero's bad.

Elf:	Do you like Miranda?
Caliban:	Alright for a human.

Elf:	Have you ever met your father?

Caliban: NO.

Elf: Do you like elves?
Caliban: No, no, no, no, no, NO!

Elf: Do you want to kill Prospero?
Caliban: YES. (Thinking to himself.) Having first seized his books or with
              a log batter his skull, or cut him with a stake, or cut his neck with
              a knife, never fails to possess his books for without them he is but
              a sot. But I say magic his spirit to command, they all do hate him.
              Burn his books so he is powerless. The beauty of his daughter
              overpowers, but I have not met this woman. I just want to kill
              him. KILL, KILL, KILL.

PROSPERO 2

Child: Why did you not let Ariel go when you said you would?
Prospero: Caliban might turn against me.

Child: What did you do with Caliban's mother?
Prospero: She was mortal.

Child: Why did you use your power against Caliban?
Prospero: He is evil, he is pathetic and above all he is a liar.

Child: Why did you enslave Caliban?
Prospero: That I cannot answer.

Child: Why do you hide your powers?
Prospero: To save them for a tragic day!

End

Child: But this rough magic I here abjure: and, when I have required
              some heavenly music – which even now I do – to work mine end
              upon their senses, that this airy charm is for, I'll break my staff.
              Bury it certain fathoms in the earth. And deeper than did ever
              plummet sound I'll drown my book.

Chapter 5

Avenue Junior School

'Be not afeard' – Producing *The Tempest* with Juniors

Margot Fawcett, Frank Gallagher, Carol James, Ian North, Dorothy Waite

Avenue Junior School, one of the two inner-city schools involved in the Project, decided to do a full-scale, formal production of *The Tempest* with staff taking responsibility for aspects of production and children from all year groups as actors, dancers and musicians. The original text was retained, albeit reduced, for the school aimed to demonstrate that primary-aged children can understand and deliver complex Shakespearean language in a way that not only conveys meaning but retains the phrasing and the rhythm of the verse. This was a whole-school effort that made heavy demands on resources and called for positive commitment from all staff and children, especially since most rehearsals took place after school. *The Tempest* was presented in school, at the Shakespeare Festival and toured to other primary schools. *Editor*.

CONCEPTION

It was a casual comment which precipitated us into a full production of a Shakespeare play with a cast of over a hundred children aged 7 to 11. At an early meeting of schools taking part in the RSA's pilot 'Shakespeare Project' someone said that it had to be borne in mind that Shakespeare's text was very difficult for children in their early teens, because of the language barrier.

This made us think about the implications for our 7–11 juniors. In our medium-sized (300+) Junior School we routinely introduce Shakespeare together with other pre-twentieth-century authors. In fact, an assembly question on 23 April is as likely to receive the reply, 'Shakespeare's birthday' as 'St George'. Various groups have acted scenes from plays including *Romeo and Juliet*, *King Lear* and *Macbeth*, Act V of *A Midsummer Night's Dream* and a shortened version of the latter. Although staff had every intention of using story, drama, speech, art, craft and writing, we wanted something more extending than just a whole-school 'project'. Perhaps the barriers erected by adolescents through early sophistication might not exist for our less self-conscious juniors. Why not, we thought, approach a Shakespeare text by the most obvious route, stage a whole play?

Two questions presented themselves: which play and who would take part? The second answered itself: as many as possible across the school. The first question, surprisingly, not much more difficult; the Histories were good for numbers and action but we preferred to avoid more war; the same was true of *Julius Caesar,* the only possible Roman play; of the tragedies a version of *Macbeth* was to be seen by the upper years, *Romeo and Juliet* we felt was better left as a whole play until later and the rest were beyond the age group. The comedies offered more and *As You Like It* and *Twelfth Night* were possible though limiting of numbers. However, we thought the fragile, bitter sweet quality of each might be better savoured by a more romantic age-group. We briefly considered *The Comedy of Errors* and *The Merchant of Venice.* The first, if the 'difficult' text is cut, leaves little but action, while The Merchant's basic theme needs very careful handling. *A Midsummer Night's Dream* was obvious but would not be breaking new ground, which left *The Tempest.*

The action of The Tempest would, we thought, offer excitement and amusement and its fairy-tale quality would appeal to our children. There would be layers of thought and numerous themes to be explored: treachery, justice, revenge, magic, power, love and, above all, joy and reconciliation triumphing over bitterness and anger in rebirth. Further, there were outstanding opportunities for music and dance involving large numbers of actors. By this time we had determined on full performances, first to the most important audience, ourselves, then to parents and others, four performances in all. From that point our problems and their solutions whether technical or dramatic became, in fact, educational and the more we worked at the play the more there seemed to be to explore, so that the final performances, although a culmination, were also points on the road to further knowledge.

Our school productions are normally team efforts which have been successful in bringing a range of talents and ideas to bear. This was going to be necessary to some extent if groups from throughout the school were to be rehearsed and the cast were to be large. In the event we had three main directors, a further director for the Masque, a music director and a chief designer, all assisted by most other staff. Fortunately, the tensions were creative and not even verbal blows were exchanged.

Introducing Shakespeare in detail to children was the main objective so it was determined that the production would wherever possible reflect his period, thus putting him in context.

THE SCRIPT

The most important job to begin with was, we felt, the preparation of the script. If we could get that right then everything else would follow, as indeed it did. We hoped to be able to use Shakespeare's text without 'modernizing' but we wanted the play condensed so that both players and our own young audience were not overtaxed. Two of us spent time in the summer holiday going through the play independently, cutting and planning. At the start of the Autumn term we sat down together to pool our ideas. We went through the play, line by line, and arrived at a consensus. In fact we found our policies were very largely in agreement and moot points were soon sorted out.

Lines that we felt were well beyond the children's understanding, by virtue of maturity level or experience, were removed, plus anything that was coarse or bawdy and some words that emphasized the bestiality of Caliban, which we thought inappropriate for child actors. We cut out the dialogue of the scenes featuring the King and his companions completely as it seemed rather tedious for this age group and replaced the action with movement to music. The storm and the betrothal masque were also planned as movement and music but a few lines were later retrieved to guide the audience.

Two very long important speeches of Prospero's were not cut but pre-recorded by the actors on tape and played as 'voice-overs' to avoid the responsibility and anxiety of having to remember such long and significant passages. Prospero's Epilogue speech was treated as separate from the action and delivered live by Prospero Number 4 (see below). Prospero's story of his brother's treachery and his own exile was shown as a mimed vision using Prospero Number 3 while Number 1 related it to Miranda. This helped to clarify it for an inexperienced audience, avoiding their joining Miranda in slumber, gave scope for additional actors and introduced an Elizabethan theatre 'dumb show', furthering learning. It is, of course, not impossible that Shakespeare's own production used the convention at this point. We were at all times concerned that our performers should not lose their enjoyment by feeling overburdened.

The next problem that presented itself was how to prevent children adopting a special 'poetry voice' when faced with blank verse to read. Even those with high reading ability are sometimes apt to treat poetry as so different from prose that they lose all meaning. We decided to circumvent this tendency simply by having the script printed out as though it were all prose. We were confident that if we took care to maintain the rhythms and balance in our cutting, then Shakespeare's poetry was strong enough to take care of itself. We were not disappointed.

We considered which aspects of the play we wanted to highlight, what we and the children thought it was really about and how the title, characters and action related to each other. We confirmed that for our school it was a play about forgiveness on an enchanted island, about tempests or bitterness, anger and vengeance finally allayed by the powers of pity and mercy.

After the cutting the script fell naturally into twelve scenes, which we named according to their place in the story, and the final production ran for one and a half hours. We maintained a flexible attitude to the script throughout rehearsals and a few further small cuts were made where we found an actor simply could not relate to a particular phrase and deliver the meaning. But this was never a major problem.

REHEARSALS

The task of auditioning was time-consuming and somewhat complicated. It had been decided to fill speaking and major dance parts from Years 5 and 6 (aged 9–11) while drawing sailors, waves and minor spirits from the younger (aged 7–9) children. Trying to match the many interested children from Years 5 and 6 with, firstly, the speaking roles and then with the roles that demanded good movement as well as voice, was a difficult process. Perhaps surprisingly, having three directors helped rather than hindered this procedure. When dealing with large numbers of auditions it was of great benefit to have discussion and confirmation of casting.

Over a period of several weeks we listened to children individually reading aloud and then in various combinations reading sections of the text. In the spirit of the Elizabethan theatre we had no gender boundaries on characters. Our 'cross-dressing' was, however, from female to male. The decision to double up on all the named characters was made at a very early stage and was to some extent philo-sophical as well as practical. A part such as Prospero or Ariel, even in a reduced state, was a huge undertaking for a child of primary school age. We had, in fact, four Prosperos, three speakers and a mime. On a philosophical level, in the play, as in our school life, the whole is the sum of all its parts and often more: so it proved here. Every role was treated in the same way, in as much as it had at least two performers, even though some roles could easily have been undertaken by one child. This expedient also ensured that as many children as possible were involved in such a bold endeavour. However, the combination of actors extended the range in some parts. The Ariel of the first half was appropriately frisky, even slightly aggressive, while the second-half Ariel brought out an essential, affective rela-tionship with Prospero.

Tackling the words, the syntax, the conceits of Shakespeare's play was neces-sarily a quiet, almost private undertaking. This experience has been likened by some to learning a new language. We would disagree with this and rather liken the process to acquiring and using dialect. Many of the words are familiar and are used in similar ways, but there are others which are exclusive to the area from which the dialect comes and consequently new and yet others which are the same but have unfamiliar uses. The acquisition of this 'dialect' at an early stage in re-hearsals was essential.

To this end each director took groups of children, whose characters had a col-lection of scenes, and by careful reading, discussion and analysis drew out the meaning in the text and ensured that both actors for each part understood what they were saying. In addition groupings of children were tried out and the best fit found in each case in terms of compatibility of voice quality and body size. The way the play was divided up between actors was largely decided at this point, so that children only had to learn the lines in their part of the play, but knew the re-mainder in some detail.

As a teacher this was an extremely interesting and rewarding episode in the total experience. Opening children's minds to Shakespearean English, such an important and innovative component of the language, is a delight and a privilege. For the actors it was an initiation; a recognition that the language of Shakespeare was rich, expressive, comic, tender and relevant.

Rehearsals proper took place over a fairly long period of time using, initially, staff and pupils' own time in the lunch hour and after school. At this point actors were called in the groups of characters selected earlier and both 'halves' of each character attended all rehearsals. This meant that once moves were decided, ab-sences did not disrupt rehearsal schedules, since one actor could stand in for the other, making the correct moves, but reading from the script. Moreover we quickly established the habit of walking a scene through with the set of actors who were not actually going to learn that section of the play. This enabled us to have in-built understudies, the value of which was proved overwhelmingly when, at one evening performance, a main character was taken ill literally seconds before his entrance.

Before the scripts were discarded, the play was blocked out. Once that had been done, the actors relinquished their texts with amazing speed and with a deal of confidence. This was a consequence both of the careful textual work done at an earlier stage and the huge enthusiasm displayed by the children for their task. When the named characters were joined in rehearsals by the many children, some from Years 3 and 4, who were performing mime and dance scenes, it became necessary to utilize school time. Dealing with a nearly full length play and a large acting area was not an easy assignment for adults or children of whom over a hundred were involved in all.

It was a great boost to the play in its finished form when the children were able to perform selected scenes at the Shakespeare Festival in Groby Community College. At this point the actors were suffering that self-doubt that can worm its way into all performances. The directors were emphasizing the triumphs as the project progressed, but the children, the actors, needed a dispassionate audience to confirm their achievements and encourage their efforts.

This fillip at Groby was of especial benefit to the comic scenes. Sitting in the audience , prompting, one felt and saw the actors' confidence growing and then become radiant as they enjoyed the glory of positive reaction from a largely adult audience. They knew now that they could do it – all of it – and so did we, as directors. We all returned with renewed vigour to the task in hand, that of our complete and rounded-out version of *The Tempest*.

MUSIC

In setting the play in its historical and artistic context it was natural, where possible, to use music of the period. This posed a problem with some scenes, especially the opening storm which in our production was almost entirely in dance and movement. We could find no contemporary music to fit adequately. The same was true for the courtiers' scenes which, again, were played in mime and movement. It was necessary to compromise and look elsewhere for music for these scenes while using, for example, airs and dances by Dowland and Allison as other incidental and introductory music.

Songs by individuals were also a possible problem and except for Caliban's drunken 'freedom' song we avoided solos by assisting actors with a small backing choir. Though settings of 'Full Fathom Five' and 'Where the Bee Sucks' are common, few are appropriate for junior school voices. Indeed the-well known Arne setting of the latter, familiar to older teachers, causes particular difficulty. At this point we made a find. The settings by Robert Johnson for the first recorded production of *The Tempest* (1611) were performed on Radio 3 within days of each other. These were printed with a single melody line in an Appendix to the Arden edition and further, our local music library had a piano setting in an aged copy. (Note: *The Songs for Shakespeare's Plays*, edited by T. Maskell Hardy – 1933. The book was long out of print, though not quite out of copyright, but Messrs

Schirmer very generously allowed us to copy without charge.) The settings seemed eminently fitting, tuneful and 'the real thing', but could they be performed by a small junior school choir?

There were great misgivings at two melodies apparently far more suitable for an adult early music ensemble than junior school voices. However, a small group of nineteen children battled manfully, and the melodies were learned by heart. When it came to our first run-through with the cast, it was totally dead and the piano accompaniment was very out of keeping with the rest of the play. It would have been impossible to sing unaccompanied, so first of all we tried a solo flute playing the melody line. This was lost in our hall, so we were back to square one.

The choir numbers were then increased by the addition of the nine Spirits, who were all previous choir members. This gave the children more confidence and a former Avenue pupil played the melody on the viola. This also freed the teacher to conduct the choir.

To our great surprise and delight it sounded magnificent. We could almost imagine the original being sung with lute accompaniment, and the choir were extremely pleased with the end result. Others may say it was due to our experience, but we feel a lot of luck went into it as well.

MOVEMENT AND MUSIC

The scenes planned as movement with music, namely the storm, the King of Naples on the island, the False Banquet and the Betrothal Masque, developed extremely well once appropriate music was found. The most difficult of the four proved to be the Masque and it is fair to say that it often seems slightly awkward in a professional production. For the other three, music was needed that was dramatic in sound, with some qualities of magic and mystery: music that did not sound too reminiscent of any particular period but had a feeling of directness and some variety of tone to fit different parts of the action.

The immediate storm music that came to mind was Benjamin Britten's *Sea Interlude* from *Peter Grimes* and in the event his *Sunday Morning Interlude* was found to have the right elements of brightness followed by menace for the False Banquet scene also. For the scene in which the sleeping King is nearly murdered by his own brother, something sinister and panicky was needed to match the action of Shakespeare's text; again Benjamin Britten met the requirements with his *Passacaglia*.

Planning the movement and fitting it to the music proved straightforward and the children learned to use the changes in the texture as signals for changes in the action. To simulate the movements of sea and wind in the storm we had a team of waves, the youngest children in the play, attacking the outside of the ship and nine Spirits of the Island harrying the sailors and passengers inside, while Ariel directed operations from a high point on the vessel. In the later scene the Spirits produced and laid out the Banquet and then, on the courtiers' approach, whisked it away again while Ariel advanced, cloaked and threatening.

Having a mixture of dialogue and movement gave variety and balance to the production and eliminated some more of the problems of learning words. As noted above, the dramatic music was linked by incidental period music before the play and live music for the songs, all giving added colour and atmosphere. A lively Italian court dance on crumhorn and tabor proved entirely appropriate for the Neapolitan clowns. Individual live players provided the music of the island by which Ferdinand and the comic characters are enticed, thus complementing the dialogue.

THE MASQUE

The children taking part in the Masque were drawn from those who did not have major roles or who had changed their minds about taking part and, although enthusiastic, lacked skill in movement. The story of Persephone was chosen because it is fairly easy to portray and follow as a mime, and as a fertility myth it fits the context.

At the initial meeting an advisory dance teacher worked with the children suggesting various movements to fit the story. Children were chosen to portray Persephone, Demeter and Hades and the remainder were, in turn, plants and trees, a passage to the underworld and underground creatures. Once the music was selected from Vivaldi's *Four Seasons,* we were able to begin to link our movements together.

The masque was fitted into the main play by selected dialogue spoken by the Masque characters at the beginning and end of their sequence. We were generally pleased with the final result and felt that the children taking part not only appreciated being part of the production but also learned a lot about commitment, perseverance and working together.

COSTUMES

Costuming the play was an enormous job and was done by one member of staff as overall designer and wardrobe mistress with a team of assistants who were very willing but had limited skills. The producers decided on Renaissance Italy as the period for the costumes since this would fit the context of the story well and looked easier to make than Elizabethan dress. A collection of illustrations from the school library was made to provide starting points.

With actors sharing roles, costume became a necessary part of identification. Players were sometimes able to share a costume, but variations in size and shape meant that a number of things had to be made twice in the same fabric to enable the audience to identify characters correctly. The amount of measuring, cutting, dyeing, pinning and sewing was phenomenal.

Designing for Ariel and Caliban was a particular challenge and colour schemes were chosen so that Ariel and the Spirits reflected the pale shades of mists and sunlit spray, the waves were represented in dark blue and green and Caliban was more earthbound in greens, browns and black. All these were costumes with a lot of movement in them though the aim with Caliban was to make him look like something covered by weed or scales. The King and court were resplendent in richly coloured velvets and satins with soft matching hats, while Prospero's cloak was in a fabric that shimmered with a darker mystery.

The making of the costumes was very daunting in the early stages but it proved both creative and rewarding as it progressed and the results achieved added a rich layer to the final production.

STAGING, LIGHTING AND TECHNICAL

The first problem to be solved in setting the stage was how were we to give the impression of the action taking place on different parts of the island? Of the two possible solutions of having a central stage with differing sets or dividing the stage area into separate sections, each to be identified with one area or aspect, we chose the latter. This was partly because of the physical shape of the long school hall in which the play was to be performed and also partly due to a convention which we had built up over a number of years. This was using the whole of one side rather than an end as the stage and having scenes taking part in different areas along the length of the hall. Finally, a fixed stage curtain was used to conceal the inner part of Prospero's cell.

We chose to have three clearly defined areas, plus the centre of the stage on to which action could spill over, and which had obvious implications, such as entrances, for the dramatic staging of the play.

There was one other major consideration before we could begin and that was the needs of the audience. Having no raised seating and with a very long stage front there were potential problems with actors being unseen. In order to improve sight lines the seating was slightly curved, and in the centre of the audience, for the first three rows, a clear circular area was created for the delivery of specially significant speeches and the Epilogue. Finally, two of the acting areas were partially raised by the use of staging.

When producing the play we had, somehow, to distinguish Ariel's and Prospero's ethereal magical powers and qualities. This was largely achieved by adding an extra dimension of a third layer of height using towers placed on the staging, plus lighting effects. Some of the speeches and commands were given atop a tower. As the smaller children, especially, had to look up over the other actors' heads, this gave a focus removed from the action on the ground. Lighting only the actor and the top of the tower while the rest of the stage was in darkness added to this separatist feeling. Further, by pulsing the lights during storm or rapid action scenes, the impression of the character appearing/disappearing/re-appearing almost at will added to the aerial illusion. The confidence of the children balancing on the top of the tower, while imperiously commanding all around, substantiated the power inherent in the character.

The flexibility and adaptability of the staging design was proven when part of the production was presented at a different venue. The actual staging area was reduced and transformed from being a shallow stage with a long front area into a narrower, deeper one. The concept of dedicating areas of the stage to symbolize different areas of the island translated well. The children were able rapidly to identify with 'their' part of the stage, boosting their confidence and thus easing the transition from one venue to another.

CONCLUSION

We knew the university evaluation team would tell us something of our children's responses but would, of necessity be selective. This was an enormous project demanding huge resources of time and energy. Therefore, we continually asked ourselves, 'What are the children learning? What have they learned? Is it worthwhile? Is the cost justified?'

First there were the standard benefits of performance drama – disciplined effort, poise and confidence, use of imagination, role play, developing memory skills, projection and delivery, accepting and using direction, co-operation and a sense of shared achievement. The children shared in the various problems of staging, setting, and role building and they certainly gained insights into production techniques, including the logistics demanded by a large cast, rapid changes of scene and continuous action.

However, it was the approach to Shakespeare which was of specific interest and here we were continually gratified. Admittedly, we had cut the text but as noted above the lines were purely Shakespeare's. The language difficulties seemed to evaporate in the action of the play while, as indicated, the verse was allowed to work for itself. Individual words or phrases were explained, often by the children, and from tone and cadence it was clear that what was said was understood. This was no mere parroting. The same was true of the action. The structure became clear, from the storm opening and the flashback exposition, to the introduction of characters and groups and their alternation. Entrances and exits were clearly seen as dramatically and practically necessary – in our case for costume and player changes at least – but also to forward the plot. The full-length production enabled children to appreciate the dramatic impact of the storm opening followed by calmer exposition as a story, alone, would not. As one child gleefully said, 'That'll wake them up to start with!' Similarly, the clowns' plot was seen to echo at a debased level the original court plot (shown in mime as Prospero described it) and the renewed treachery among the courtiers.

Clearly, Shakespeare was accessible to these children through performance and, within limits, the language problem could be overcome. Above all, there was that collective sense of achievement and it was indelibly associated with Shakespeare.

If *The Tempest* was the unifying element it was far from being the whole of the school's work during the RSA Shakespeare Project. The Theatre in Education company's performance of *Macbeth* was, perhaps, better appreciated and understood for fitting into an existing context and considerable follow-up work was done. Stories from a number of the plays were read through the school, producing art and craft work, writing, and classroom drama. Some classes in Years 5 and 6 studied and performed scenes from *A Midsummer Night's Dream, The Merchant of Venice, Hamlet* and *Macbeth*. Of their own volition, a group of older children read paperback editions of some of Shakespeare's plays in their library reading lessons – for pleasure.

There was, however, still more. The 'Animated Shakespeare' videos shown on television were a bonus gratefully accepted by the whole school. Other incidental benefits have been numerous and are still coming to light. A parents' evening shortly after the performances brought a great deal of enthusiasm, not least from parents whose children had *not* performed. Knowledge of the play and words was by no means confined to performers who, as is usual among this age group, seemed to pick up everyone else's lines in entirety. Remarks such as an interval comment of, 'Do you understand it? ' 'Not all of it but it's great isn't it?' by two 9-year-old spectators suggest positive responses transcending the difficulties. Children are continually 'spotting Shakespeare' whether play, poem or mention.

A most important aspect has been the imaginative transport into the play's world, where speculation about Prospero's magic, Miranda and Ferdinand, the island's past and future, what happens to Caliban or Ariel went beside discussion of production practicalities such as who would play Stephano in Shaun's absence. That imaginative re-creation has, of course, included, partly by direction, the moral aspects of the play, in particular justice, mercy and reconciliation. Again, this taking into the self of the features of story through dramatic work in heightened language is an essential part of aesthetic, linguistic, imaginative and even spiritual development.

In a sense, these apparently incidental benefits are, perhaps, the most important. If Shakespeare is opened up so may the other riches of literature, art and music. This is what has justified the enormous expense of effort, energy and time. We shall continue to work at Shakespeare in all ways and especially by acting him.

Be not afeard; the isle is full of noises,
Sounds and sweet airs, that give delight and hurt not.

SCENE PLAN FOR *THE TEMPEST*

Scene	Title	Action
1.	The Storm	Music and movement
2.	Prospero's story	Dialogue and mime
3.	Ariel's story	Dialogue
4.	Arrival of Ferdinand	Dialogue and songs
5.	The King of Naples	Music and movement
6.	Caliban meets the clowns	Dialogue
7.	Ferdinand and Miranda	Dialogue
8.	Caliban's Plot	Dialogue and song
9.	The False Banquet	Music and movement
10.	Prospero's Power	Dialogue and Masque
11.	Prospero's forgiveness	Dialogue and song
12.	The Reunion	Dialogue
End	Epilogue – final speech	Speech and closing music

Chapter 6

Kirby Muxloe Primary School

The Shakespeare Project – A Whole-School Approach

Mike Thompson, Linda Weir, Sue Freeman, Ann Palmer, Anne Watts, Janet Thomas, Sue Gammon, Lynne Grindlay, Juliet Gasser, Elspeth Myles, Sue Trigg, Katherine Liggins, Clare Mulholland, Patsy Ryder

Kirby Muxloe Primary explored the possibility of introducing Shakespeare to every year group in one school. Consequently, children throughout the school, including 4 -year-olds in reception, were introduced to some aspect of Shakespeare and his plays. The account focuses mainly on the introduction of *Twelfth Night* to the early years with examples of emerging writing and art work. How the work related to the requirements of the National Curriculum is clearly stated, bearing in mind that the Project took place before the revision of the requirements for each subject area. The work of the children in Key Stage 2 is described briefly to indicate the range of possible approaches, including the use of resources from outside the school. *Editor.*

INTRODUCTION

As a school we had two main objectives in embarking on the project:

1. To raise the pupils' awareness of Shakespeare and his work as something to be enjoyed.
2. To use the works of Shakespeare to explore relationships.

We had three working groups, Upper Junior (Years 5 and 6), Lower Junior (Years 3 and 4) and Key Stage 1 (Reception and Years 1 and 2). All groups used drama as a starting point but each group approached the project through different plays. The whole project was brought to a close by two performances of *A Midsummer Night's Dream,* one given by Keystage Theatre and the other by Thornton Primary School.

All groups contributed art, craft and written work to the exhibition held during the Shakespeare Festival at Groby Community College but performances were only given within school.

TWELFTH NIGHT – AN EXPLORATION BY THE EARLY YEARS

The early years' group used *Twelfth Night* as a vehicle for exploring storms and feelings of loss. We intended to talk about these, paint pictures and possibly write a little. It very soon became apparent that we had taken a major project on board!

We started with a drama session, introducing Viola and Sebastian on board a ship in a dreadful storm. The children made a storm using sheets of material and adding sound effects. They worked in four groups, each evolving their own storm. They then came together and used all their ideas to make one big storm. We then developed the idea of a boat in the middle of the storm with Viola and Sebastian on board. We split once more into small groups to discuss how the twins felt and how they could be rescued. Suggestions were both practical – 'Send for the life-boat', 'Throw a rope' etc., and fantastic:

'Send for Thunderbird 4.'
'Why Thunderbird 4?'
'Because it can go under water.'

The children, even the youngest, could identify with Viola and Sebastian.

'I would be frightened.'
'I felt sick and cold.'

Paintings were bold and adventurous. Boats were built with a variety of materials. Captains' logs were written and tickets issued for voyages to a wide range of destinations.

After several sessions covering similar ground we sighted land. There was much discussion as to where it could be. Australia, France and Skegness were popular suggestions. Eventually the children were told they were in Illyria. The Year 2 children then made posters and travel brochures showing the delights of Illyria. They drew maps and used map references to devise a game of 'Find Viola'. Staff discussed the possibility of introducing Illyrian maths (i.e., different bases) but unfortunately by this time SATs were bearing down on us so the National Curriculum took precedence.

After a break the pupils were introduced to the main inhabitants of Illyria – Olivia, Sir Toby Belch and Duke Orsino. For the Reception and Year 1 children this began a flurry of castle building and royal life with many banquets being acted out. The Year 2 pupils embarked on letter writing to Olivia and Orsino and built an intricate and detailed model of Olivia's house with a pipe cleaner Olivia, clad in black, sitting reading.

The sub-plot of Malvolio, Sir Andrew Aguecheek and the yellow stockings was not introduced as the main plot proved sufficiently difficult to explain to 4-year-olds. When the whole story was revealed all the children appreciated the complications of Viola's cross-dressing. They all accepted the conventional view that 'Mummies can't marry mummies, can they Miss?'

As staff, we looked at the work done by the children during the project and related it to the requirements of the National Curriculum. Following is a list of the attainment targets achieved in different subject areas.

Mathematics	Map references	AT 4/1
English	Accounts of journey	AT 3/2
	Ship's log	AT 3/2
	Role play – 'How I felt.'	AT 1/1-2
	Listen to story of *Twelfth Night*	AT 2/2
Science	Energy sources for ships	AT 4/3
Technology	Building ships	AT 2/1, AT 3/1
		AT 4/1
Geography	Talk about other countries	AT 2/1
	Make map	AT 1/2
	Make weather chart	AT 1/2
	Work of crew	AT 4/1
	Reasons for journeys	AT 4/1-2-3
History	Ships present and past	AT 1/2
Music	Sounds of storm using body and percussion	AT 1/1
Art	Paint and draw storm pictures	AT 1/1, AT 1/2
PE	Move as a ship in storm, individually and in groups	KS1 Level 1
	Water safety	KS 2

After the project finished, children were still introducing characters and Illyria into their play. References to Shakespeare and his plays are much more frequent than before the project.

One day recently, out of the blue, a 5-year-old looked up from his work and asked,

'Who did Sir Toby Belch marry?'
'Maria.'
'Oh good.'

Yes. Shakespeare is alive and kicking in our school.

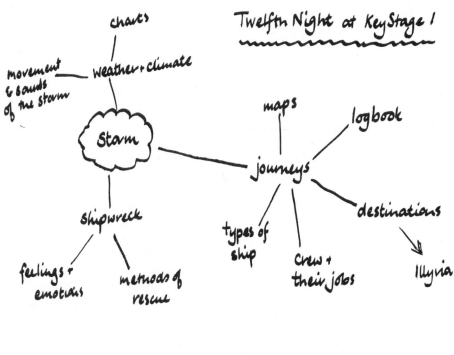

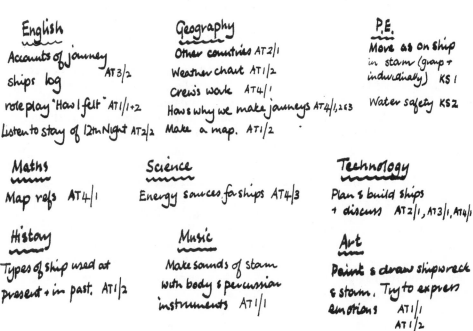

Figure 6.1 *Chart of cross-curricular work showing relationship to the National Curriculum*

LOWER AND UPPER JUNIORS

A group of 93 Year 3 and 4 children chose to look at a theme of loyalty and responsibility using *Romeo and Juliet* as a focus.

The children were grouped in families each with a suitable name – Vermicelli,
Valpolicelli, Campese etc. Each family worked out a family tree and made a set of
rules of conduct. They also drew a map of their territory. We talked about gangs
and they wrote stories about them. The children really identified with their families
and we produced a tableau in the hall.

At this point we introduced the story of Romeo and Juliet. Rick Lee, the advisory teacher for drama, worked with the children, asking them to collect evidence
about two murders.

This was developed further in the classroom with the children writing reports
from the point of view of one of the characters and re-telling the story as a cartoon.

There was an enormous amount of discussion and the children became very involved in Shakespeare's language. The culmination of the work was a presentation of *Romeo and Juliet* with each family depicting one of the key scenes from
the play.

The project generated great enthusiasm. Several children went to the Haymarket
Theatre professional production of *Macbeth* and all the children watched the
Keystage Theatre production of *A Midsummer Night's Dream.* 'It was just as if
they were just talking to me,' summed up the children's reaction.

The Upper Junior group explored *Hamlet* from the point of view of serving people
living in Elsinore Castle. The pupils played the roles of cooks and servants preparing a banquet for the royal family and guests. They became very involved in
the menus (16 courses!) and in working out the quantities needed by such a large
assembly. At a crucial time, Polonius appeared in the kitchen, called the servants
together and told them that the King was dead. He had been found in the garden,
where he had gone to have an afternoon nap. Apparently he had been bitten by a
snake. The cooks were then asked to prepare a funeral supper to replace the cele-
bratory banquet. The cooks and servants worked in groups on different courses for
the meal. As they did so, a gossip (teacher in role) went from group to group
spreading rumours about Claudius, Gertrude, Hamlet the Prince, Ophelia, the
death of the King, the Norwegian invasion threat and so on. Since these people
and events had a direct effect on all living within the castle walls, the pupils in
role became engaged in the themes, people and turmoil of the play.

The pupils in Key Stage 2 also visited the Swan Theatre and The World of
Shakespeare in Stratford. They watched performances by Keystage Theatre of
Macbeth and *A Midsummer Night's Dream* and they worked on the mechanicals'
play, giving impromptu performances to the rest of the school. The class teacher
responsible for the upper juniors concludes:

I really enjoyed the Shakespeare Project and the opportunities which it gave us. Although
initially apprehensive, the children thoroughly enjoyed their introduction to Shakespeare
and the different elements we explored. They particularly learned a lot from the visits of
the Keystage Theatre group (which really brought our work to life) and also through their
own experience of acting and the consequent opportunities to dramatize a section of *A*

Figure 6.2 Romeo and Juliet, *cartoon synopsis. The children were asked to draw the six scenes which they felt told the story*

Midsummer Night's Dream. I think the Shakespeare Projectwas extremely worthwhile and provided us with many ideas and opportunities for further educational investigation.

Chapter 7

Ratby Primary School

King Lear – Making Shakespeare Relevant

Anne Joyce

Anne Joyce, through a range of activities, explored *King Lear* with her mixed-ability class from Years 5 and 6 in Ratby Primary. She sought to give the major themes meaning in terms of the children's own lives, and to relate the language of Shakespeare to their own use of language. In particular the children closely examined the family themes, making comparisons with family situations from their own experience. *Editor.*

The Shakespeare Rap   *By Year 5 and 6*

Shout his name – let's do the Shakespeare rap
He's the one who can bridge the generation gap
All stand up
If you know his name
Everyone's heard of Shakespeare's fame
Shakespeare, Shakespeare that's his name
Stop and listen to what he says
People flock to watch his plays
Everyone do the Shakespeare rap Shakespeare
Shakespeare the Shakespeare rap
All join in to bridge the generation gap
Remember the one who found true fame
Everyone shout Shakespeare.
Shakespeare is his name.

PRELIMINARY IDEAS

In considering which play to introduce to my mixed-ability class of 9–10-year-olds, it seemed that *King Lear* would offer opportunities for exploring relationships amongst families – present day and past, thereby linking into work on personal and social education. My first thoughts were that we would make comparisons via mirror images, with King Lear standing on one side of a mirror and a present-day father on the other side i.e. the reflection. Each father would only be able to look into the mirror with the help of the character who has sole charge of the mirror – the FOOL – a character who on the outside may appear to be foolish, idiotic and frivolous but is really a much deeper, understanding person who can *see* things as they really are. The FOOL would have the power to turn the mirror to face a certain person or to lead a person through the mirror and look at things from a different point of view. It is ultimately the FOOL (who is timeless and ageless) who would have the control over the two fathers to allow them to stand back from the mirror and also see things as they really are. In my preliminary thinking, therefore, the following framework emerged on which I could base a classroom project:

King Lear		Father
	mirror	
+ Family		+ Family

FOOL

1. **Declaration of love – vanity of Father figure**

King Lear	*Father (Mr Blues)*
Daughters' proclamations of love	Birthday presents – large and visible – small (personally chosen)

2. **Relationships within the family**

King Lear	*Mr Blues*
Visiting relatives Discomfort + denials of love	Short stays with different members of family – inconvenient/in the way

3. **Illness**

King Lear	*Mr Blues*
Wandering in wilderness Loyalty of friends	Hospital visits Old folks home

PRELIMINARY MEETING WITH ADVISORY TEACHER FOR DRAMA

My initial intention was to explore *King Lear* (see above) to compare past and present day family situations in order to promote the children's personal and so-cial education. For me it was important to make comparisons with the children's own situations at home, offering a good opportunity to explore their own family relationships in the context of the play. The following plan of action was adopted by the advisory teacher for drama and myself for approaching the play:

- Get to know King Lear – a person who already knows him gives us some information about him and his family. Information is passed on in a variety of ways. The Fool (teacher in role) is the character who expresses strong opinions of the King.
- Bringing the play up to date – relevance to modern day. A person known as the Worrier (teacher in role) arrives on the scene. He has the task of direct-ing a modern-day version of *King Lear*. He has no knowledge of the play or of making films and asks the children for help.
- Comparisons made by the children. They give the Worrier's boss sugges-tions of why *King Lear* does or does not work set in modern times.

INTRODUCTORY SESSION

We asked the children what they thought was meant by the word 'kingdom' as this would be an important word in the work we were going to do. Various ideas came from the children. They then split into groups and drew pictures of things to put on our large map of the Kingdom (large sheets of blank paper Sellotaped to the floor). The children drew palaces, forests, animals and people and placed them on the map. We were then told that a messenger from the King wanted to speak to us and that it would be advisable to take a 'token of esteem' to the meeting. Children discussed what they could take and drew them. A small group of children acted as guards and we were summoned to meet the messenger. Children did not show enough 'respect' and 'reverence' to the messenger the first time so had to think about their actions and were summoned again. This time the King's messenger told us of the King's dilemma. He was getting old and had decided to pass his Kingdom on to his three daughters but did not know how to share his Kingdom out fairly. He asked the children for advice. Their task before the next meeting was to choose some spokespeople who would put forward the children's suggestions.

During the week before the second drama session with the advisory teacher present, the children and I discussed the situation in class and suggestions were put forward. Spokespeople were chosen and children wrote what they had learned of the King.

SESSION TWO

The children reported back their four suggestions for sharing the Kingdom amongst the three daughters. All the children wanted to speak at once. We introduced a rule, as in a court of law, that a person should stand if they wanted to speak. Any criticisms were blamed on the scribe of the suggestions (teacher in role). The children were then informed that none of their suggestions would be acceptable to the King as he had since made up his own mind about how to divide up his Kingdom. The children were told of the King's plan. He had decided to ask each of his daughters how much they loved him and to give them a share of his Kingdom depending on their declaration of love. The children were shown parts of the answers given by the princesses to the King. It was explained that the language was 'different' because of the time element and because of the status of the princesses in society. The children were told the princesses' names and position in the family – youngest, middle, eldest. A variety of clues was given out as to the personality of the princesses when they were told their names, e.g. Goneril sounds rather hard/harsh, Regan sounds manly, Cordelia sounds softer, more feminine. Children divided into three groups to read the speeches of one of the daughters. Dictionaries were used to help with words that were unusual or the children were unsure of. Within the groups the children managed to cope very well on the whole and created a fairly good picture of the three daughters. Perceptive comments were passed by some. For example:

> That daughter said she'd give up her eyesight for the love of her dad ...
> What person would do that? She doesn't sound right to me ...

> This one said she couldn't love him more than her husband – I don't think her husband would be too pleased if she did.

The children were then asked to choose someone from each group to represent the princess and interpret her speech for everyone else. This caused some upset initially – children found it difficult to choose one representative, some found it difficult to swop from being 'in role' situations, others felt very self-conscious while some were frustrated with the lack of participation of others. We gathered the children together and tried to persuade them to co-operate with one another. It took quite a long time before the three groups were ready to proceed.

We watched one group at a time make an entrance to declare their love for the King. It became obvious which individuals felt inhibited by the situation but the majority responded well. The three groups made a regal entrance including trumpeters, maids, guards and servants. A spokesperson for each group declared the love of the princess for the King in their own words. All the declarations of love were delivered in a formal, respectful manner suitable for the presence of a royal person. When they had been made it was made clear that Cordelia's group was to be banished from the Kingdom and they dispersed. The other two groups were situated in different parts of the hall and told to prepare for a visit from the King and his army. Preparations started to be made for a royal visit.

Meanwhile, the Cordelia group was advised to send spies into the two other groups to gather information about the sisters' actions and to keep Cordelia informed of the actions of her father. These children took their spy roles very seriously and managed to move in and out of the groups without drawing too much attention to themselves. The other two groups busied themselves with preparations for the King.

The session ended with a discussion concerning these preparations, considering what food to prepare and the quantities, what clothes would be worn, what weapons would be used in conflict, what entertainment would be necessary. The children were to research these things before the session the following week. They were also told that certain children had extra information that the others had no knowledge of as yet, referring to Cordelia's spies.

Between the drama sessions, the children researched materials related to the Shakespeare Project. We devised a worksheet which would highlight further information about the period in which King Lear is set and about the actual characters in the play. The information was collected together by the children and then presented to the rest of the class via a talk and the showing of pictures. The presentations were followed by discussion.

SESSION THREE

The children were split into six groups and each group was given a large sheet of paper to draw on. They were asked to draw pictures to represent the following:

- King Lear
- Cordelia
- Goneril
- Regan
- Goneril's servants
- King's soldiers

The children discussed the pictures and all took part in drawing and colouring them. As a whole class we then shared our ideas and discussed the preparations which would be made for a King and his followers.

The children were then given some lines from a speech made by Goneril, namely:

His Knights grew riotous

and

You and your fellow servants
Put on what weary negligence you please.

It was interesting to note that it was not the most capable people in language who coped with Shakespeare's language. It did seem to come easier to those who enjoyed role play situations and could adopt a role with more ease. Very few of the children felt they could not cope with the language. In fact they all actually enjoyed reading and reciting it.

The children were asked what they thought the words meant. Various interpretations of the word 'riotous' were given. Those the children seemed to like most were 'behaving badly' and 'getting into brawls and fights'. The word 'grew' was discussed and the children came to the conclusion that the Knights were not, as yet, riotous, but were getting that way. The children wondered why the Knights had started to act in a riotous way and various suggestions were made including (i) they were tired, (ii) they were hungry, (iii) they were sick of marching, (iv) they were sick of the King, (v) they were sick of each other. When the children were asked what they thought Goneril was saying to the servants, surprisingly most of them guessed right, even though many were unsure of the meaning of the word 'negligence'. It was decided that Goneril meant the servants should behave in such a manner that made them unbothered, tired and uncaring.

The children then split into separate camps – the soldiers or the servants. Once this was done, they were asked to form two 'human pictures' akin to ones which had been drawn earlier. One was to be of a marching army and the other of servants during preparations for a visit. The children tried to form two groups of stationary people to represent these pictures. The first attempt was a little dull and uninteresting but the second attempt was much better. They were then asked to become 'moving pictures', so that the action took place. The army of soldiers, tired and hungry, finally reached the palace to be met by a lethargic group of servants. It was interesting to witness the children's reaction to one another. At first they were rather reserved but following further discussion reacted in a very 'rebellious manner' – although managing to stay within role and within control.

Before the final drama session with the advisory teacher, the children were asked to consider why Goneril should want to stir the soldiers up and encourage the servants to react in such a manner. The children had reacted much more positively in the third drama session and coped very well with the role play situation. Only a few children had found it difficult to portray themselves as characters in the play.

The class became involved in research in the library, looking for information on the following topics and recording it in writing and drawings:

- What type of food would be given to the King and his party? Make out a menu. Remember you are preparing food for 100 soldiers. How would the food be cooked and presented?
- What money was used at the time the play was written? Draw some coins.
- What would the princesses and the King look like? Describe them in words and pictures.
- Describe what the soldiers would look like and what weapons they would carry.
- What do you think the palaces would look like? Describe them in words and pictures.

SESSION FOUR

The children were reminded that the servants and the soldiers were about to meet
at Goneril's palace. They were asked to consider what might happen next and how
the story might end. The majority thought there would be a fight between the servants and the soldiers which would lead to a lot of bloodshed at the end of the
story. Most of the children agreed that King Lear would die at the end; some felt
he would be killed while others felt he would die of old age. Differences arose,
however, when they discussed what happened to the three daughters. Most of the
children's arguments were based on logical reasoning.

Examples of the views of the children on the development of the plot:

- We think the King dies of a broken heart because he misses Cordelia and
  wants her back. But he is stubborn and won't ask her back. Regan goes off
  to Spain and Goneril rules the land and makes the people miserable. Regan
  will come back and kill Goneril.   (Louise and Daniel)
- We think that the King will be murdered by someone and everything will
  get out of hand and lots of people will die. Regan and Goneril will pair up
  together against Cordelia then when she is out of the way they will fight
  each other for power.   (Lewis and Ibrahim)
- We think the soldiers will win the fight and Goneril will poison the King so
  that she can have all the land. When Lear dies he is glad because he is such
  a sad man without the love of Cordelia who we think is really his favourite
  daughter. We think Lear regrets sending Cordelia away and would rather
  die without her.   (Mary and Nicola)
- I think there will be the biggest war you have ever seen. The King died of a
  broken heart.   (Leanne and Jenny)
- We think there will be a big war between Goneril and Regan. We think he
  died of stress at old age. It would be nice if Cordelia came back but we
  don't think it has a happy ending.   (Robert and Rachel)

Rick drew a picture on the blackboard of a church and a cemetery, with a sole
figure standing amongst the gravestones. He told us that when we entered the hall
this would be the setting for the end of the story. The children and I discussed
how we would enter such a place and it was decided that it would be with great
caution, anxiety, suspicion and interest. When we reached the hall the sole figure
was represented by Rick and the inscriptions of various headstones were placed
around the hall. The children tried various ways to get information from the figure
in the cemetery. They approached him as individuals, in groups and as a whole
class. Some tried to use force. None of their tactics seemed to work. Finally we
asked him to show us what happened to the characters who had died in the story
and who were now buried in the cemetery. Rick used some of the children to re-
enact the final moments of certain characters' lives before they died. This was
captured on video. The children were able to gain a great deal of information from
these enactments – especially as they could watch the video over again and pick
up more pieces of information and look at the inscriptions on the headstones in
more detail in an attempt to interpret Shakespeare's language.

CONTINUING TO WORK ON *KING LEAR*

The children worked in small groups trying to build up a character profile for some of the main characters in the play. They used all the evidence, research and information they had gained over the past few weeks as well as reading sections of the play itself which they felt might help them to understand the characters a little better. This is where they needed a lot of teacher guidance so that they chose to discuss relevant pieces of the text rather than pick some in a very haphazard fashion. Once they had some understanding of the main characters and of the plot the language did not appear to be too much of a barrier to them. They started to 'think' in a Shakespearean way and even to 'speak' in a Shakespearean manner.

Many children enjoyed learning short quotations by heart and saying them aloud to each other. King Lear's final words were learnt and remembered by most of the class because we read them and discussed them so many times. The children enjoyed trying the words for themselves and relished the sound of them even though they may not have understood their full meaning.

The children enjoyed discussing and building up a character profile for the main characters. I found they were often very loyal towards the character they had discussed and researched. Even the evil deeds of some of the characters were excused in an effort to support them. The children experimented with role play situations. They tried to portray their character in a modern day setting. This stimulated a great deal of discussion and the children tried to think of all the reasons why a person may turn out to be the way they are. Various suggestions were made:

- the childhood and upbringing of a person
- the love or lack of love from family
- sibling rivalries
- lack of self-confidence
- low self-esteem, or in the children's words, 'didn't think they were any good at anything'
- bad experience with other people
- looking for attention

Once a personal profile for the main characters was completed the children were better able to discuss what might happen at the end of the story. They looked back at their original suggestions and altered them as they felt fit. With more evidence and a greater understanding of the people involved and of the plot, the children made some very revealing and sensitive suggestions for ending the story. One group of children actually 'guessed' the ending as it actually happened and were able to suggest some very sensitive and complex reasons why certain characters acted the way they did.

ACTING OUT THE PLAY

We acted out the story of *King Lear* as we had come to approach the play for an audience of Year 5 and 6 children. The performance contained the following scenes:

Scene 1	Discussing what was meant by a kingdom and putting
Scene 2	The King's messenger calling the people together to tell them the King had decided to pass on his Kingdom to his three daughters
Scene 3	The proclamations of love by the three daughters to the King, leading to the banishment of Cordelia
Scene 4	The King's visits to his daughters Goneril and Regan and the upset caused between the King and his soldiers and the daughters and their servants
Scene 5	The King in a mad rage feeling bitter, angry and alone
Scene 6	The death scenes in the cemetery and re-enactments of what had led to all the main characters' deaths

The children also tried to portray parts of the story in a contemporary setting and in groups they attempted a modern version of certain sections. For example, the proclamation of love scene was transferred to a modern-day father at Christmas time asking the children how much they loved him. Some of the children gave outrageous replies in an effort to gain very big Christmas presents whereas others gave much simpler answers. Through further work in this area, we shall continue to explore some of the feeling and relationships which came out of the play itself. It seemed that the project could be never-ending!

EXTENDING THE EXPERIENCE

In further discussions, the class looked closely at the daughters' declaration of love to their father. The children had mixed feelings about the responses the daughters made. Most felt Cordelia had been foolish to say what she said because she must have known how it would hurt her father. Also most of the children could see no wrong in telling 'white lies' as long as no one got hurt by them. When asked how they would have reacted in the same situation most of them decided they would have been more like Goneril and Regan and given similar replies.

The children were then asked to think of a more modern-day situation which could be used as a parallel to the declaration of love scene in *King Lear*. They split into groups of seven or eight to discuss the situation and decide on the main idea of the scene. The children in each group then went on to act out their scenes. There were four main scenes within the class:

1. Mum and Dad are taking the children on a shopping spree to 'Toys R Us' but before they go the parents ask the children to tell them how much they love them.
2. It is the children's birthdays soon and Mum and Dad call the children together. They tell them they only have so much money to spend and before doing so would like to know how much each of the children loves them.
3. It is nearly Christmas time and money is a little short now that Dad has lost his job. Before making out their Christmas list Mum and Dad ask the children to tell them what they think of them.
4. An elderly mother writes to her two children and their families explaining that she would like to go on holiday with one of the families. The families discuss the problem and try to decide who she should go to and for what reasons.

All the children watched the different groups act out their scenes and then discussed who really loved the parent or parents in the scene and for what reasons. This discussion continued at great length and comparisons were continually made with the *King Lear* situations. The children then wrote a story based on one of the drama scenes that had taken place. I was very pleased to see how understanding and perceptive the children were within their stories.

King Lear had provided a strong stimulus for:

- Discussion work
- Devised group drama scenes
- Role play
- Creative writing
- Art work

PARTICULAR CLASSROOM ACTIVITIES RELATED TO THE EXPLORATION OF *KING LEAR*

- Pictures to represent 'The Fool' – old-fashioned and present day.
- Front page newspaper headlines representative of something dramatic related to the King Lear story.

     e.g.   KING FOUND WANDERING ALONE
             ROYAL SOLDIERS DISMISSED
             KING DIED OF BROKEN HEART

- Interviews on tape – news reporter interviewing someone who witnessed a certain event, e.g. the death of King Lear.

- Embroidered messages – children designed and embroidered a message for a loved one.
- Epitaphs suitable for characters in the play.
- Listening to different pieces of music and choosing something suitable to represent certain scenes from the play.
- Planning menus suitable for a royal feast and making menu scrolls.
- Maths work in planning a Royal Feast for the King and his 100 soldiers.
- Making model castles out of junk materials and out of plaster of Paris.
- Writing speeches in a Shakespearean style – short speeches to a friend, enemy or loved one including some of the words commonly used by Shakespeare.
- Having some fun with the language devising Shakespeare style quotations:

  Hath thou a coloured mark to put upon the parchment within mine hand?
  (Pass me a crayon.)
  Shall I – thy servant – wipe away the used dust from thine board of darkness?
  (Shall I rub the blackboard?)
  I admire from a distance the shining globes which fall neatly from yonder lobes.
  (I really like your ear-rings.)
  Is that the distant cry of babes in glee?
  (Is it playtime yet?)

- Reading the storyline of other Shakespearean plays.
- Research on Shakespeare himself – information placed on the computer program and added to whenever any new information was discovered.
- Making a collection of Shakespearean works and creating a display in the classroom.
- Large pictures and paintings of Shakespearean characters – these were based on children's drawings which were then enlarged using the overhead projector.
- Devising sound effect stories on tape to represent certain scenes from the play – for instance making storms, wind and the sounds of a marching army.
- Television news reports based on certain scenes from the King Lear story – these were updated and put onto video.

Chapter 8

The Casket Makers – *The Merchant of Venice*

An Account of Advisory Work at St Peter's Church of England Primary School, Market Bosworth

Rick Lee

At the time of the Project, the LEA was undergoing profound financial changes in which money was being devolved to schools and the authority's departments were developing into self-funding agencies. The drama and dance advisory team was still intact, however, and was able to make a strong contribution to the Project. Teachers' appreciation for this support is reflected in their accounts. Primarily concerned with involving mixed-ability classes of any age in an educative experience through a Shakespeare play, Rick introduced an approach through role play that would directly engage the pupils. The following account describes his work on *The Merchant of Venice* in Market Bosworth Primary to illustrate his approach. *Editor*.

'His carriage is at the corner of the street!'

In the cabinet makers' shop there was an excited fluster. Crafts folk were adding last minute touches to their finished caskets. At various tables groups of them were gathered, foreheads creased in frowns, pencils in mouths, other pens writing furiously, arguing over the bill.

'Well, how long did you spend on that scroll – you were at it for ages!'

Another group was busy selecting a wine and cleaning glasses.

'Do you think he'll want anything to eat?'

'He's at the door!' screamed the look-out in a hoarse stage-whisper.

There was a tap of a cane at the door. One of the crafts folk went to open it and greeted their customer.

'Would you like to take refreshment before inspecting your order?' she asked with an elegant politeness.

'I don't mind if I do,' replied the smiling customer.

After wine and some hastily acquired sandwiches, the customer was shown into the workrooms. He inspected the three caskets and declared them to be more than satisfactory. He asked a few questions about various aspects of the work, but seemed genuinely pleased with their efforts. There followed some embarrassing moments because the bill was not ready.

He agreed to receive their account when it was completed and said he would arrange for the caskets to be collected that afternoon. After further praise for their craftsmanship, he bid good-day and departed. Amid the sighs of relief after he had gone a slightly querulous voice was heard to say, 'I don't know what all the secrecy was about, what does he want them for anyway?'

A week later in the foyer of a large mansion a group of young men and their friends and servants were gathered, waiting to gain admittance to the young lady of the house who was with her friends in a room off the foyer. The young men knew that the huge mirror to the right of the door into her room was in fact a two-way mirror and that the young women in the room were at that moment inspecting and commenting on the young men's appearance, their clothes, hairstyles and general demeanour.

They didn't need the door open to hear the squeals of pleasure and excitement that this game was causing in her room and were decidedly not looking forward to their entrance into that giggling nest. They had all brought presents and regarded each others' offerings and supporters with interest.

The door opened and one of the young ladies came out to announce the name of the lucky suitor – or victim!

Half an hour later a group of 8- and 9-year-olds were heatedly discussing the reasons a suitor might give for choosing the lead casket, one which Portia would accept.

They were the same group of children who had made the caskets and eventually presented a bill to Portia's deceased father's solicitor; the same children who had prepared and enacted the suitors wooing the haughty young lady surrounded by her giggling friends. These children have no problem with Shakespeare. They've struggled with his poetry and worried about the morality of making people go through hoops to get what other people have fixed anyway. They have talked to other children in the same school who tell them of the horrendous trouble other people in the same story have got themselves into. They know that this same Portia, who seems a rather proud woman to them, given to teasing with undisguised contempt all the young men who seek her hand in marriage, is the person who saves the life of her lover's friend by cleverly outwitting his persecutor. They have also overheard the fierce arguments raging next door in the trial of Shylock.

In other parts of the school younger children were meeting an aged magician on a mysterious island, who asked them to help him find an ugly monster called Caliban and invent fairy traps. Even younger children were worrying about who had left a baby out in A Winter's storm. They helped a shepherd and his son decide what to do with the baby and with the gold that had been left with it.

So how did this happen?

How were the children in the activities quoted above able to get so involved with these three plays and at such a level of interest and understanding?

The truth of the matter is that the assumption that Shakespeare has been abandoned by post-modernistic, non-acknowledgers of classical literature is probably erroneous. My colleagues and I in the Leicestershire Advisory team would argue that William Shakespeare has always been and always will be a great ally and a rich and ever relevant source of material. I suspect the same goes for many other teachers throughout the country.

The children involved in *The Merchant of Venice* were a class of thirty 8- and 9-year- olds. The three lessons described in detail above were not consecutive but occurred irregularly over the span of two months. I propose to use these lessons as exemplar material for a discussion of how role play techniques were used to try to make this difficult play accessible to these students.

WHY CASKET MAKERS?

When I am asked to engage children in a particular area of concern I ask myself the question, 'What is it I want them to learn?' Generally this would be strongly influenced by what I perceived to be their interests and their needs. In this instance it was simply to find out that Shakespeare could be interesting. In fact they were being used as guineas pigs by me to see if Shakespeare could be made accessible to young children.

There are a range of things I then bother about.

FOCUS

I need to identify some aspect of the material – a moment or event or question or problem that contains issues central to it. The delineation of this focus will vary depending on the group and the material, but it is merely a starting point from which other focuses can be chosen. (See Figure 8.1 which Dorothy Heathcote has used to explain the different frame distances. She stresses that every frame that creates the differences in concern *also* creates different and very subtle linguistic tracks and must *generate* talk quite differently from your 'Authority' reconstructor. This means style, vocabulary and *sense of audience* (role participant, or internal audience – the self-spectator checking on the truthfulness or effectiveness) all shift gear.) Often it is useful for this focus to be oblique. I decided that the caskets, which are central to one of the main strands of the play, would provide me with this focus and immediately saw that other essential considerations could be met.

FRAME

The next question is, 'Who do we need to be that we are bothered about the focused event or problem?' I believe that framing enables people to see the world through a variety of lenses and they are thus able to reconsider all knowledge that is presented to them. In this case there were various people in the play who are concerned with the caskets, including Portia and the suitors; but I decided that adopting the attitudes of casket makers would allow the children to engage with the caskets and their meanings in an oblique and intriguing way, with the potential of dealing with the leading characters always available. The frame of casket makers also allowed me to bring tension and intrigue into the room and provided us with a specific set of tasks to complete. It also gave me an opportunity to put pieces of Shakespeare's text in front of them. The diagram indicates that the frame need not be close to the event. In fact we could just as easily have been a group of

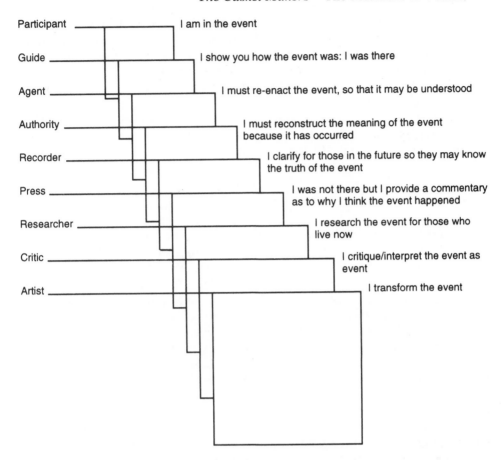

Participant — I am in the event

Guide — I show you how the event was: I was there

Agent — I must re-enact the event, so that it may be understood

Authority — I must reconstruct the meaning of the event because it has occurred

Recorder — I clarify for those in the future so they may know the truth of the event

Press — I was not there but I provide a commentary as to why I think the event happened

Researcher — I research the event for those who live now

Critic — I critique/interpret the event as event

Artist — I transform the event

Figure 8.1   *General role function in relation to frame distance. Each frame distance provides students with a different, specific responsibility, interest, attitude and behaviour in relation to an event. (Heathcote has used this diagram several times to explain the different frame distances. Taken from unpublished paper, 1980.)*

propmakers working on a production of the play – or the Venetian gutter press who have found the verses and have to run a story on the young heiress. The possibilities are endless and each one immediately puts you into the telescopic framework of the diagram so that from any starting point you can move closer or further away and these opportunities should be taken.

TENSION

Tension is essential to drama and is the engine that makes it work. The tension in this case was introduced by the fact that the instructions for completing the tasks were given by myself in role as the solicitor's assistant stressing the importance of the work, that it needed to be done quickly and that it was to be kept secret. The children were intrigued because they were not given much information and the words they had to deal with were difficult to read. In fact the whole task was odd and the solicitor's assistant was not very helpful. Later on, tension came from knowing that the solicitor was coming down the street. This was done simply through narration and strung out for as long as they could bear it. There was terrific tension in the air as he silently inspected their craft work, as he sat drinking his wine and when he wanted the bill. The tension in the wooing sessions came from the excitement of boy meets girl, from the device of the two-way mirror and the delicious anticipation of the interviews and decisions that might be made. These excitements were in both the fictional and real worlds and are the stuff of drama.

TASK

Another consideration is, 'What task will the participants be doing and have they the means to do it?' Casket making seemed an appropriate task for these children to do. The instructions came from myself in role as the assistant to the solicitor who was dealing with the will left by Portia's father. The requirements were written down and included copies of the three verses to be placed in the caskets and the inscriptions to go on their lids. The class teacher provided the materials and the children were told the time limit they had to complete the work both in the drama as casket makers and out of the drama as students. This task actually began to raise issues from the play almost immediately as children began to wonder why it was secret and what the words might mean. Very quickly they wanted to know more about the person who had commissioned the caskets and the daughter who was the reward for the fortunate suitor. They began to question the morality of such a father and were later very doubtful about Portia's manipulation of the arrangement, although the girls enjoyed the power this gave them! They were also interested to hear of the gruesome aspects of the rest of the story from other classes, but they kept their caskets and the contents secret! Other tasks created were the making up of accounts, the making of presents and the invention of questions and answers for the suitors. The cross-curricular fertilizations of role play are myriad. But, whenever I am in the middle of role play, I must always stop and ask myself, 'What are they actually doing and have they the means to do it?'

TEXT

One of the major worries for primary and secondary teachers in dealing with Shakespeare is the text. I cannot claim that all the children understood all the text they were presented with, but they were not overfaced by it. I think there were two reasons for this. Firstly there were only three small extracts to begin with and they were able to struggle with them together. Secondly, they were not told that these words were from Shakespeare, although they soon found out. I believe it was the fact that they were presented with the words in another context that required them to deal with them in a specific way which allowed them to engage in a non-threatening way, which got them engaged obliquely. Later on they would be prepared to struggle with much bigger chunks. I think the problem of the language is a bit of a red herring and is more to do with labelling and a certain style of didactic teaching than anything to do with the words. My own experience has taught me that the presentation of any text in small contextualized packets makes the whole text more accessible – and who needs the whole text? I remember the student who was struggling to learn the part of Lucio in *Measure for Measure.* In frustration I told him to just enjoy saying the sounds of the words! What a revelation, both for him and me. Suddenly he had no problem and soon after began to understand what he was saying. The problem had been in the mind-set of, 'I'm not supposed to enjoy this – it's hard'. The language is there to be struggled with and enjoyed for its rich tapestry.

OTHERS

A further matter that I bother about is how to get the children involved without them feeling stared at. I think many people, including drama specialists, overestimate people's ability to enact roles authentically. To avoid this problem I attempt to distract or intrigue children into dramas by engaging their attention with significant 'others'. This can take a lot of forms: objects, maps, drawings, and most powerfully the teacher or someone else in role. These children met the solicitor's assistant, the solicitor, Portia's butler and an older student in role as Portia. The caskets they made and the attention paid to them by the solicitor; the presents and the drawings I made of the mansion and the solicitor's carriage, all worked to stop them feeling stared at. This was even so when the suitors were on display in the foyer, because we drew them first, which afforded some protection for the boys, who were merely representing those young men.

TEACHER IN ROLE

Teacher in role is a device that needs a book all to itself, but in this context, as we have already seen, it is a useful way of providing a powerful and intriguing 'other' for children to pay attention to. It also allows the teacher to feed information and set up tasks. It is not acting, but adopting the attitude of a solicitor's assistant who has to ask a group of casket makers to do a discreet job. This does not require much in the way of acting skills, although it does mean that you have to become a competent manipulator of the signing in a space. By this I mean make significant alterations to the space or your behaviour and possibly your costume. In fact in theatre terms the minimalist approach is most useful, because the single or limited use of props makes them more obviously significant. This can be simply that the chairs and desks are arranged differently. For example, the door between Portia's room and the foyer was indicated by two chairs. However, this is not a big problem because we can agree that I have got a cane in my hand as I tap on their imaginary door. In this case there was no cane and no door – our collective imaginations will do this magic with ease. The important word to remember here is 'significant', because we can only agree that something is there in our fictional word when we give it attention. This can be done by agreement e.g. 'Shall we have the door here – or here?', or I can indicate its significance by estrangement, e.g. I place three caskets on a red cloth on a table in the middle of the classroom either before the class enters or, if I really want to make a big drama out of it, I can set up the class as hidden observers, who see me as a servant (or a cheating suitor!) bring the caskets in and give them an air of importance or secrecy or contempt.

Teacher in role gives me a lot of flexibility and opportunities, but probably the most important rule is that I must teach the children about my ability to come in and out of role at any moment. This protects me and allows me to retake control if I think the class is getting out of hand, but more importantly it allows me to show that role is most useful as an analytical tool. In the safe laboratory of role play I can move in and out of different roles altering the focus of the investigation and all the time questioning and wondering what we need to consider next. This is the process I call role shifting (see Figure 8.2) – moving between the real world and the fictional world – from me as teacher through negotiator to a twilight world, where I wonder what I might say to casket makers as a solicitor's assistant – to the full role. All the time I am shifting I am teaching the mercurial fluidity of this form, which is available and richly present in our lives.

I am also aware of three levels of role status. As solicitor I am a higher status than the casket makers, so I must be careful not to treat them with contempt. I must value their craftsmanship as a different skill to mine. By far the most useful status is the intermediate role. The solicitor's assistant is only doing his job; he's passing on information that he does not necessarily understand. This allows him to worry about deadlines, but it throws the responsibility of completing the task onto the casket makers. A lower status, such as the new apprentice, can also be useful because he can ask a lot of very innocent, even seemingly stupid questions, which acknowledges the power and knowledge of the crafts folk, yet can subtly challenge their thinking.

CONVENTIONS

Teacher in role is actually a simplification of an enormous palette of alternative devices, which are available to the teacher and to the children. In her seminal article *Signs and Portents* delivered at a Theatre in Education Conference as long ago as 1980, Dorothy Heathcote identified over 30 conventions or ways in which we read the presence or absence of someone. Some of these, unfortunately often used out of context as tired tricks, have become the staple diet of drama classes the world over. Still images, freeze frames and thought-tracking are probably the most popular, but these are simply catchy titles for one convention on Heathcote's list – 'Role depicted as picture: removed from actual life'. Full role is also only one convention. Hot seating is the interviewing of that full role. There are 30 or more other conventions that are used less often and I would advise anyone wishing to use role play to spend some time going through the list of these conventions and invent accordingly. The richness of the diversity is breathtaking, especially when you consider that in many schools it seems to be largely ignored. I have found that some

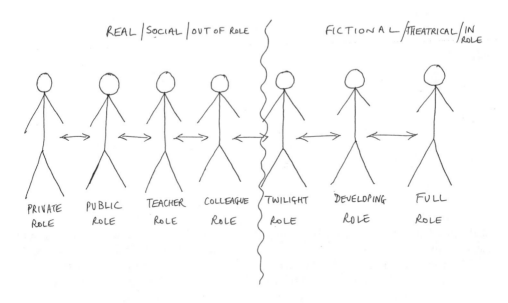

Figure 8.2   *Role-shifting*

conventions which are particularly useful do not even look like drama and can project children into fictional worlds without them feeling stared at. For example, the role of the solicitor was created from a drawing of his carriage. One of the children insisted that it must be a BMW carriage and so that was what we had. I quite often draw the person we are going to meet before we see him, or we can see him in the corridor before he comes in, or we look through two-way mirrors, or binoculars, or we become Portia's portrait painters or the cryptologists analysing her handwriting. People wonder where the ideas come from – that one list would keep you going for a long time. Coupled with the opportunities afforded by frame focusing, the experimentation in our drama laboratory can be endlessly creative.

Chapter 9

A Primary Teacher's View of the Project

Muriel Walker

I am sure that all those concerned in the process of education would agree that real knowledge rests upon a basis of practical experience of concrete things and events, and such experience is an essential element in the education of every child. From the outset the Shakespeare Project was an exciting event just waiting to happen. What did happen, and the out-reaching results, are chronicled here.

Those concerned in the Project's conception determined that the experience should not be, as many would assume, solely for those children who had reached the age at which Shakespeare is traditionally taught, but also for children in the primary sector.

When the invitations to participate were received in schools, there was no hesitation in relating them to each school's particular circumstance. No one responded in negative vein concerning the 'tender' years of the pupils involved. It was always envisaged that the material would be appropriate and relevant. Obviously interests and aptitudes of individual teachers involved would play a great part, but then this could be said of any subject taught and would apply equally to the participating pupils. Some of these latter would be as young as 4 years old.

Correspondence bearing the name 'Shakespeare' would, in secondary schools, probably be directed to the English or Drama departments. Thus, neatly compartmentalized, the Project would unfold therein. Obviously, this did not happen in the primary schools where it is usual that each class teacher tackles every subject area. Therefore the Project was more likely to have a whole-school focus. (One participating school has a teaching staff of two.) At least, each member of staff should be aware of what was happening and would benefit from sharing the experience, if only as a casual observer.

Primary teachers actively involved in the Project thus found their colleagues to be supportive and co-operative, willing to offer comment and constructive criticism. Teachers who did not initially intend to take part, found themselves caught up, carried along and swept into the current as the children's enthusiasm grew. The children should take great credit for this, as they are great communicators and sharers, given the opportunity. My personal experience was that pupils invited other teachers to 'bring your class to watch us ... it's ever so good!' and then queried, 'Well, what did you think of that, then?' thus acquiring both audience and critics in one fell swoop! This extended the possibility of securing the whole school's interest and involvement.

Before the Project began, teachers were aware of the need to make it both meaningful and accessible to their pupils. As young children develop, they encounter ideas and concepts which cannot be learned directly from everyday environment, but only indirectly from other sources. When encountering Shakespeare's work for the first time, the children would, initially, be largely dependent upon their teachers. The communication of ideas and concepts would be a joint adventure for the communicators and receivers. There was definitely always the feeling that this was a special experience for us all.

No richer source material can surely be found than the works of Shakespeare. There is such a diversity of themes in his plays that the most superficial quest is instantly rewarded. Many primary teachers, accustomed to a cross-curricular approach, looked for links with other National Curriculum subjects and found this an easy task. This is demonstrated in the account of the early years' work on *Twelfth Night* in Kirby Muxloe Primary School. Each felt that the inclusion of Shakespeare's work was more than worthwhile. Gone is the onus for justifying choice when the contributory material is part of our heritage and generally recognized as such!

The exact nature of the work that was undertaken necessarily varied from school to school. This factor could be considered one of the most valuable outcomes of the Project in that it proved that there is no clearly marked door into Shakespeare, but many entrances. All the work detailed here is very clearly child-orientated, and in some cases became, commendably, child-directed.

There was always an element of choice about the amount of commitment required by the Project. Some teachers tackled the task single-handedly, others worked as a team. In some cases the work involved whole-class participation, in others selected groups worked together. It is encouraging to note that many of the participating teachers would not profess to be either English or Drama specialists. The only requisite qualification was a desire to participate in the Project. No one was ever made to feel inadequate to the task.

Skills of interaction, communication and co-operation were learned as the children participated as whole-heartedly as only they can. The eagerness of younger children for sharing their enthusiasms was ever to the fore as they played, sang, drew, wrote, acted, listened, watched, talked and wondered while they learned 'all about Shakespeare'.

Funding for the Project made possible collaborative meetings between participating teachers from our family of schools and enabled schools to 'buy in' extra resources. Most primary schools had input of some kind from the Leicestershire Drama Advisory team, who played an important role not only in stimulating responses from the children, but in generously sharing their expertise with the class teachers. The confident enthusiasm which they brought to the schools gave teachers a much-needed fillip. It also ensured the future of drama sessions in many primary schools in that teachers both know the value of such lessons and, perhaps more importantly, are willing now to attempt to implement them. Teachers who make drama lessons part of their usual classroom practice were able to evaluate their work and to confidently reiterate the fact that such sessions are worthwhile. Other teachers were able to appreciate and acquire new techniques which will greatly add to their teaching skills. The work done by visiting drama staff admirably complemented the work of the class teachers and made their joint contributions successful.

Collaborative meetings lived up to their name. Everyone was very positive in approach. Factors that might have been seen as problems (e.g. three year groups in one class; the involvement of nursery-age children; no specialized knowledge of Shakespeare) were seen as challenges. We laughed at our mistakes, and learned by them. We shared experiences and swapped ideas. We were not just theorizing but were discussing what was actually happening in our schools and the practicalities involved. We were very often surprised by the perspicacity and perception shown by our pupils, as you will probably be when you read their work. Do we challenge them enough? Do we, because they are so young, spoon-feed them too much? We asked ourselves these questions and many more. Perhaps we didn't find the answers, but we were made to think deeply about what we, as teachers, are doing in the classroom. For most of us, this was a salutary exercise! At the early collaborative meetings, the aims of the Project were agreed. These were not solely seen as educational objectives, but as the route to achievement. What those achievements were can be interpreted from each others' sections of this book, but throughout all runs a great sense of celebration. If nothing else, the name William Shakespeare seemed to act as an integrating symbol which secured the support of all.

Primary education is all about first experiences. If we label and experience 'the first' then we imply that there are more, of a similar nature, to come. The children involved in the Shakespeare Project developed specific concepts and skills which they will use in the future. Their responses to Shakespeare are limited only by the extent of their present knowledge and experience. Both will be extended when they meet his works again. Who knows what their future responses will be? We hope that, one day, in the not too distant future, we will find out. Then we will be able to judge the success of the Shakespeare Project more fully.

Chapter 10

Keystage Theatre in Education

Macbeth for Primary Schools

Maurice Gilmour

INTRODUCTION

As part of the Shakespeare Project, Keystage Theatre in Education Company, established by Leicestershire County Council in 1985, adapted *Macbeth* to test the feasibility of introducing primary school children from an early age to Shakespeare through a professional performance. The production was toured to schools throughout the authority, but an evaluation of audience response focused on six primary schools involved in the Project – Stafford Leys, Markfield Mercenfield, Newtown Linford, Stanton Under Bardon, Lady Jane Grey and Thornton. The company members included four actors, Simon Cuckson, Ruth Hellier, Jane Perkins and Paul Waring, a technical director, Peter Jackson, and myself as director.

At the beginning of rehearsals, the company members shared their experiences of Shakespeare at school. One actor described how, in the fourth year at secondary school, her class read *Romeo and Juliet*, their first Shakespeare play. It was a mixed comprehensive but only the top set had to do Shakespeare. There was one book between three and the students voted on who should read which parts, which led to much argument and embarrassment. The play was read round the class accompanied by a lot of nudging and sniggering. The majority of the class could not follow the text, and though they had problems with the language, they were still forced to read aloud. Understandably, many were very reluctant to read and for most, Shakespeare became something that just had to be got through.

In another secondary school, Shakespeare was taught as part of English literature from the age of 11, mainly for examinations. Although the approach was predominantly academic, the teacher was inspirational because of her own enthusiasm for Shakespeare. Even so, as a student, the actor felt out of her depth and found difficulty in relating the plays to her own life.

One actor said how much like a foreign language Shakespeare was, and, when it came to reading aloud in English lessons, everybody would shout , 'Don't pick me – pick her.' Some pupils found it very difficult to read aloud but the teacher insisted that they should. The rest of the class did their best to help those who had difficulty in coping with the language. As they read round the class, the students were asked to change parts which made the play even more difficult to follow. The students had to go through the whole text of a play from beginning to end, making notes and learning quotations for examinations.

Another member of the company had not met Shakespeare until the third year in secondary school, when the teacher played a recording of *Romeo and Juliet* while the class followed the text in their books. To avoid the teacher's eye, he sat at the back of the class reckoning that the bright sparks at the front would answer any questions or do any reading that might be required. His second and final experience of Shakespeare in school was in geography when he saw the second half of Olivier's film of *Henry V* – the geography master just happened to be the school projectionist!

Despite these experiences, we agreed that the variety and scope of Shakespeare's themes, the rich texture of the language, the huge range of characters, and the wit and the broad humour fully justified his inclusion in the curriculum. We discarded any doubts that his continuing presence in the secondary school might be due to the British love of tradition, or his position at the hub of a thriving industry. Yet, given the qualities of his plays, we had to consider why it appeared that the majority of people were alienated by them at school, as long, boring and irrelevant, and avoided them once they left school, seeing Shakespeare as the preserve of a small intellectual middle class. It was felt that the plays could be made accessible and enjoyable to all students, provided teachers could find the right key. Similarly, a concern was expressed that many productions of Shakespeare alienate students because they do not engage their interest and fail to make the plays relevant to their lives. Nor did we believe that could be achieved simply by expedients such as using modern dress. Some emphasis in the production was needed to provide a direct link between the themes and the experience of the audience. The challenge for Keystage Theatre was not only in attempting to provide such a link, but also in accepting the central aim of the RSA Shakespeare Project that Shakespeare could be introduced to children from a very early age.

CHOICE OF PLAY

It was decided to present a version of *Macbeth* to children aged 7–11 years. Although considered by some schools to be a very adult play and not suitable for primary-aged children, we saw within the play many themes and situations that concern people of all ages. This view was guided by the belief that life is real and earnest at any age and that childhood is not only a preparation for later adult years. Friendship, love, power, cruelty, indeed all elements of the human condition are experienced by children. What often appears as playing or a minor difficulty in the playground is not so to the participants. We resolved to show that any play can be made accessible to primary school children, and therefore chose *Macbeth* as one that would not normally be considered suitable for this age range. Friendship and loyalty are important themes within the play and explore issues such as making friends and falling out, and facing up to the moral dilemma of when to tell on your friends and when not. The pressure that is applied to people to behave in a certain way or to undertake a certain course of action as typified in *Macbeth* is close to the world of the playground where children are often goaded into doing something that they might not want to do. In teasing out these themes, two elements within the play gave us particular cause for concern, namely violence and witchcraft.

VIOLENCE

During early consultations with colleagues in schools, a number expressed dismay or, at the very least, uncertainty about the choice of *Macbeth* because of the violence that pervades the play; the fighting, the killings, and the murders. Some talked about the need to move away from the violence seen on television screens and in the newspapers. This worried us a great deal, because the last thing we wanted was to add to any anxiety that children might have. It was also a matter of practical concern that some schools might decide against having the play because of their fears about the violence and how children or teachers might react to it.

The question of the relationship between children's behaviour and the level of violence they experience at first and second hand is often debated but never satisfactorily resolved. More often than not it is left to the individual teacher to make the decisions about what exposure children should be allowed to experience in the school situation. Some seek to involve the children in the decision-making process, while others operate what amounts to an external censorship. There is a danger, particularly in the latter approach, of trying to shield children from the issues raised by violent actions ,and, in doing so, suppress aspects of their lives that are very real.

> One of the reasons I like this play is because it doesn't end with a happy ending. All the stories that you usually see say things like, 'and they lived happily ever after'. It's not though, because all of the main characters die ... Personally I like a lot of blood and guts in a film, and I recommend this for anyone a bit like me, but if you don't I say stay as far away as you can!
>
> (Pupil, 10 years old, Thornton Primary)

Then there is the 'play violence' that is not always understood. Children are discouraged from participating in pretend fights that range from fisticuffs to sophisticated war games in the belief that to allow it to pass unchallenged will result in aggressive behaviour at a later date. Children are encouraged to believe that to commit a violent act against some other person is wrong, although they will perceive that society considers it acceptable under certain circumstances, e.g. the righteous war, the apprehension of a criminal. It is at the centre of man's dilemma, the struggle between natural inclinations and intellectual moral conscience which has been epitomized by the conflict in the philosophies of Locke and Hobbes. It is a struggle that is with children, not just adults, although many would like to think otherwise, ignoring the message of *Lord of the Flies*. In hanging onto the belief in the innocence of children, we relegate them to a lesser sphere, denying them their true thoughts, feelings and relationships. At the very least we ought to acknowledge that children have to deal with violent feelings and situations and that they are capable of coming to terms with them, especially if they receive the right kind of support. In this we found what we considered to be a justification for not rejecting *Macbeth* as a play for primary school children. What we did reject was the prurient violence that is often promoted by the media as a sensation within itself and with no appropriate context; hence the avoidance of realistic images in presenting the fighting, murder and killing.

WITCHCRAFT

We debated the witches as much as the presence of violence within the play. In seeking to avoid presenting them as the children might expect witches to be presented, namely as rather nasty, bent, unpleasant women with strange garb and habits, we hoped to challenge the expectation and say there is another way of looking at this. The reluctance to present the witches as women also stemmed from a determination not to provide the audience with a stereotype role model.

How could a link be established between the children's lives and the force represented by the witches in the play? The problem was never resolved completely. Possible interpretations emerged like mushrooms and some were tried out in rehearsal. One saw the witches as part of Macbeth's unconscious thought process and a concrete manifestation of his inner life. But how could this be reconciled with Banquo's recognition of the witches? Only with some difficulty I hasten to say. It's very difficult to muck about with Shakespeare. His plays allow you to change and alter and subtract, but only in a way that is acceptable to the true form and content. You soon know when you've played a wrong note. Finally, however, an idea emerged.

Looking at the school playground, we considered the ritual of children's games, the patterns of movement, the themes, the chants and songs. In them there is a world of ritual magic where intoning certain words results in particular behaviour and actions. Like the witches' rituals, so too have children's games and songs been passed down through the ages. The original meaning of the words and the games may have gone, but the rituals remain unchanged. There is, too, the power of children's groups over the individual, a power which is more often than not exercised in a friendly, playful way, but which can take on a more sinister character. So it was that the witches connected *Macbeth* to the world of children's games, at once playful but with dark undercurrents. Although some children and teachers in the audience were disappointed that the witches were not bent, cackling women with pointed hats and warts (and it is interesting that following the production, some of the children's art work depicted the witches like this!), the interpretation generated a lot of interest.

THE TEXT

Allowing for an adequate get-in and get-out and the demands of a primary school timetable, the running time for the production had to be under an hour, otherwise the bell would go in the middle of a scene, the dining hatch open or children depart home. *Macbeth* in less than an hour. This entailed careful editing that would retain the main themes, characters and as much of the original text as possible. When you try to cut a Shakespeare play you find out very quickly how cleverly interwoven are the thought processes, the events and the words. Selecting particular themes and characters helped with the editing. Macbeth, Lady Macbeth, Duncan, Banquo, Macduff, Malcolm and the witches were retained. Some characters such as Lady Macduff, the murderers and the doctor made brief appearances. Others including Donalbain and Lennox disappeared completely. In order to give continuity to the story line, there were occasions when speeches of deleted characters would be spoken by other characters in the play. For instance, the lines announcing that Macbeth is to be made Thane of Cawdor are, in the adaptation, spoken by Duncan and not by his emissary.

Though determined that the play should stand by itself and that the children should be exposed only to the language of Shakespeare, we were concerned that the story line might be obscured by the cutting and the number of roles three of the four actors were playing. The fact that children as young as seven (in the event children as young as six) would be watching the play had to be taken into account. Also it was inevitable that some would be slow learners having problems with language. Although the intention was to challenge the children, it would be unhelpful to bewilder them, and thereby fail in the attempt to introduce Shakespeare in a way that they would enjoy and find interesting. Therefore, at certain points in the production, short pieces of narration were inserted to keep the audience on track. They may not have been needed but they were so short and in keeping with the tone of the production that they felt part of the play.

We sought to maintain a clear story-line. Macbeth, Banquo and Macduff were depicted at the outset as three friends fighting for Scotland and honoured by King Duncan, a friendship betrayed and destroyed by Macbeth, encouraged by Lady Macbeth. First dishonoured by killing the King, Macbeth is seen almost helplessly to succumb to the need to kill all those who might challenge his position and authority. The terrible consequence of friends falling out. Interwoven in the tragic story of a flawed hero was the theme of ambition, the desire in men to climb to the pinnacle of power and become 'king of the castle'. The witches were child-like beings with magical, sinister powers. Their rituals resembled a children's playground and their apparently innocent prophecies were underlined with a strong sense of menace. Their distorted game of 'I'm king of the castle' established one of the main themes of the play.

THE STYLE OF PRODUCTION

Working in schools is always a challenge because of the variation in the acting area, ranging from a hall with a well-equipped stage to a classroom with no technical equipment at all. In seeking to avoid the problems of the end stage presentation which would only be viable in schools with stages and which meant many children being a long way from the action, the play was presented in the round. Because of wide variations in technical equipment, blackout and time for setting up, no stage lighting was used and, in the event, no recorded sound.

This style of presentation has its drawbacks. It is difficult to address all sides of the acting area equally and the danger exists of the children catching sight of their friends opposite and collapsing into a Mexican wave of giggles and hysterics. The audience can see every movement and every loose thread. On the other hand, because of the close proximity, the actors have the opportunity of developing a close relationship with the whole audience. In this particular production, the four sides of the auditorium were never more than four rows deep and a raked effect was achieved by the use of gym mats, benches and chairs. The children could see easily and the rake created an enclosed theatre arena within the space.

Because of the limitations of having only four actors and the concern that the children might not be able to follow the language, we considered presenting the play as a rehearsal with the actors in the role of actors stopping intermittently to discuss and argue about the problems of the text, the costume, the witches and so on and thereby share the difficulties with the children. However, we finally decided that the play should stand by itself, leaving the children to grapple with the plot and themes and to unravel the language as best they could. Some short pieces of narration were introduced but only to clarify the ambiguity caused by the cutting of the text.

One actor played Macbeth only while the other three played three or four roles each. The actors were clearly visible to the audience at all times, either on stage or in an aisle, changing role, waiting to enter, or playing an instrument. Actors shared the changing of their roles with the children and the main roles were named in an appropriate fashion. Use was made of freezing the action, in particular when soliloquies were spoken, so that lines could be directed towards a visible character or group of characters. Apart from helping the children to follow the thinking of the speaker, this theatrical device produced strong, dramatic images such as the one of Macbeth, as he spoke of murdering Duncan, with his face very close to the still image of his trusting king.

Partly because of the absence of a stage manager, the actors met the children as they came in and showed them to their seats. When the audience were ready, the actors stood four-square centre stage facing outwards, announced the play formally and then launched themselves into it. The play was ended in a similar way, with the actors as a group in the centre of the arena.

DESIGN

The set design was very simple. Each of the four aisles represented a particular location in the play – Macbeth's castle, Duncan's castle, the witches' haven and a combination of Macduff's castle and England. A stand held the masks, costume and artefacts of the characters related to one of the locations. The four dressed stands created an environment as well as a base from which the actors could enter. A small stage rostrum in each corner could be brought on to provide an extra level or a seat. The four locations gave the children additional clues for identifying the characters. The actors worked as a team, helping each other when a role required an actor's presence in two or more corners at the same time!

Because of the demands of playing many roles and not having any time to don full costume it was essential to find a basic costume that would be neutral, give a flavour of the mediaeval period and of the present, and suggest the warrior and the playground. The final design was a black tunic, with black leggings or tight trousers, Doc Marten boots and a studded leather harness. Bodhrans, large drums of Celtic origin, were worn on the back by three of the actors and brought to the front to use as shields in the fighting sequences or as drums. These bodhrans, looking like pale harvest moons, were awkward to manage at times but they gave a Celtic feel to the costume. The Doc Martens looked strong and warlike and were light and quiet to move in. They did not work so well for the Lady Macbeth role but they were acceptable even then. The leather harnesses were ideal for holding the drums and beaters and gave the basic costume a military look.

Additional costume that could be put on quickly and easily was worn on top of the basic to represent each character. For Duncan a large cloak and a crown, for Macbeth, Banquo and Macduff plaids of different colours, for Lady Macbeth and Lady Macduff over-garments of the same colour as their husband's plaids and a simple night-gown for the sleep-walking scene, for Malcolm a short cloak and a prince's crown, for the murderers black SAS-type balaclavas, and for the doctor a white coat and leather Gladstone bag. In each case, we searched for an image that would speak directly to the children, which could be put on easily and allow freedom of movement.

The witches wore two- or three-sided half-masks so that a face was always turned towards each section of the audience, even when there were only two actors in role. The masks contrasted with and distorted the childlike movement, playground rituals and sing-song voices to create an eerie, unearthly effect.

Props were chosen for their simplicity and clear imagery. For instance, before killing him, the murderer enmeshed Banquo in netting and in following scenes, the actor used this, pulled tight over her head and face, to represent the ghost. Other props included a gold medallion to symbolize the Cawdor inheritance, a candle for the sleep-walking scene, two tree branches for Birnam Wood, and the crown, which was treated as the all-important symbol of power throughout the play. At first, the beaters for the bodhrans were used as daggers, to further abstract the violent scenes, but teachers and children in the first two weeks of the tour were so adamant that the daggers should look like daggers, that we began to use more realistic-looking wooden daggers.

MUSIC

There was no technician's finger to press a switch at will so it was decided that any sound should be live. In the event the sound developed as an integral part of the production and served to create atmosphere, to reinforce the action and heighten feeling. The main instruments were a violin, played by Ruth, and three bodhrans played by Paul, Jane and Simon. The production began and ended with a Celtic-type folk dance in which the actors played their instruments as they danced. The actors used the bodhrans as drums to provide background for processions, announce a change of scene, and represent violent battles. The antagonists fired off percussive sounds which were received as blows from swords. Voices and other percussive instruments were used, some for special effects. For instance, the murderers of Banquo and Lady Macduff advanced on their victims using a scraper, which sounded very like the threatening sound of a rattlesnake. It was the instrument, increasing in speed and volume, that effected the killings. Ruth carried the violin in the witches' scenes and used it as her voice or to heighten tension. It was the violin that introduced the children's song, 'I'm king of the castle', and echoed it, sometimes with voices, through the play. The violin underscored the slow agonizing death of Duncan and sweetly established the innocence of Lady Macduff and her child with a Celtic air.

FORMAL EVALUATION

Two questionnaires tested the reaction of pupils in six primary schools to the play and their knowledge of Shakespeare in general. The responses were recorded in three particular age bands of 6/7 years, 8 years, and 9/10 years. Only one school did not show the ages of the children, so that their findings were not included where age differentiation was given consideration. Over 300 pupils completed the two questionnaires (Appendix 1). The children were responding to one particular production, but, even so, the results give an interesting picture.

The first evaluation sheet dealt with the general attitude of the children towards Shakespeare and they were asked to choose between 'Yes' or 'Don't know' or 'No' to ten questions. Eighty-seven per cent of the children said they were looking forward to the play, but only 55.2 per cent because they knew it was a play by Shakespeare. Yet, after the performance, 79.6 per cent said they would like to see more plays by Shakespeare, 87.9 per cent said that Shakespeare is not only for adults and 64.6 per cent thought that his plays should be taught in school. If we look at the responses between the three age bands, there is surprisingly little difference, although there is more uncertainty over whether Shakespeare should be taught in schools.

Children's understanding of events in the play were tested in the second questionnaire with a further ten questions to which they could answer, 'True', 'Don't Know' or 'False'. The results showed a good level of understanding. For instance, 81 per cent affirmed that King Duncan made Macbeth the Thane of Cawdor, 75.2 per cent that Malcolm escaped to England, and 65.5 per cent said that Lady Macbeth did not see Banquo's ghost. There was some uncertainty over two of the statements made, one concerning the prophesy of the witches to Banquo and the other asking if it was Macduff who was crowned at the end. The statement that the witches told Banquo he would become King of Scotland was rejected by 55.3 per cent of the children and only 35.5 per cent said it was untrue that Macduff was crowned King at the end. Apart from these responses, however, the children showed a good understanding of events in the play. Again, there was little differentiation in responses between the three age bands, although it was the uncertainty in the younger age groups which brought the percentages down in the last two responses quoted.

The limited nature of the evaluation warns against accepting the results as proof of any theory, but it does give a strong general indication of the attitude of children towards Shakespeare and whether his work would be appropriate material for primary schools. The children seem to be in little doubt, and in the response they make they may be asking that educators should re-consider what might be deemed too difficult for the primary school curriculum.

FOLLOW-UP WORK

In addition to the evaluation exercise, teachers involved their classes in a range of activities after seeing the play which gave opportunities for pupils to express what they had experienced and to develop their thinking further. It became clear that Shakespeare could be used as a springboard to develop understanding and skills in many areas of the curriculum. The pupils were involved in language work through discussion and writing.

David Ashfield, deputy head of Newtown Linford Primary, describes the response of his school to the production:

> If Shakespeare is to be introduced to primary children, then Macbeth seems a good choice. Short by comparison with most other plays, it lends itself to be reduced further without ruining plot or theme .... A feature of the small primary school is its flexibility; knowing of the Keystage Theatre venture, we leapt back 250 years or so to change the next term's history project from the Victorians to the Tudors so that Macbeth could readily be incorporated into our work ... we also used the opportunity to explain a major characteristic of language – that it is constantly changing. New words come into the language, old words get forgotten, grammatical usage alters. Also few plays are written in verse these days. These things are barriers to appreciating Shakespeare. We applauded Keystage's decision to use the original words, rather than a 'translation'.
>
> The play, when it came, captured the attention of the junior children and their initial response was positive and favourable. They had a brief opportunity afterwards to talk with the actors. It has to be said that their first questions concerned technical problems and overall impressions rather than deeper, moral dimensions! Later discussion with the children revealed that the plot was very well understood, and that everyone agreed the Macbeths got what they deserved!
>
> We did not wish to direct the children into adult-orientated artificial responses, and most of the children preferred an artistic response to their experience rather than a written one. Castles and witches featured prominently in their art work, and it became clear that the supernatural and conflict aspects were strongest in their minds.

Examples of written work from all the schools abound, some concentrating on accounts of *Macbeth*, others containing a critical element, but all revealing a good understanding of the framework and detail of the play. Activities involved graphic design, art work, written composition and computer skills. For instance a number of children were encouraged to compile a page of newsprint that demonstrated their knowledge and understanding of the play. Several examples of this are shown. Many classes depicted scenes or characters from the play through pencil drawing or paint.

One of the most interesting activities emerged from Newtown Linford Primary and is again described by David Ashfield:

> Our work had taken a further direction after I had noticed a group of boys on the swimming coach playing a card game – one of those games with warring mythical figures with various ranking points for attributes like 'strength', 'skill', 'courage' and so on. I suggested to the group that they might like to make a similar game based on Macbeth.

This was enthusiastically received. In Daniel's words,

> On Friday we started them in the library. We gave ourselves jobs. Joshua was good at drawing so he drew the pictures. I did the side panels and then Andrew took over that job. The side panel has six characteristics or categories – weapon skill, strength, speed, bravery, intelligence and toughness. Robert and Joe did the side panels I coloured the pictures in.
>
> This is how you play. Deal out the cards upside down, then give out the trump cards. Choose the person who starts. He chooses one of the characteristics on his top card. The one who has the highest number in that characteristic has won the cards. Carry on until someone wins all the cards.

The deputy head continues:

> What Daniel's account doesn't mention is the intense discussion and co-operation that went into the making of some 30-odd cards and the standard of draughtsmanship that the boys (mostly 9-year-olds) set themselves. Probably as many cards were made then rejected for not being 'up to scratch' for various reasons. In deciding the attribute rankings, the boys needed to discuss the various characters – Macbeth, Banquo, Macduff, Malcolm and so on. They brought in extra features on the cards – like Birnam Wood, Banquo's ghost – to give additional twists to the game. I quote the Banquo's Ghost Rule:
>
> > 'If Macbeth's card and Banquo's Ghost card are played, Macbeth gets 3 for the called skill – weapon skill, speed, strength, bravery, intelligence, toughness. But it only affects Macbeth'!
>
> Shades of the play itself. It should be mentioned that the boys received practically no guidance from staff, except occasionally as advisers on authenticity – for instance 'yes' to a battering-ram card (-1 to the castle owner!), 'no' to a crossbow (marginal perhaps). There was much consultation of books on history and warfare.
>
> After many busy group sessions we had to call a halt to the card-game making as it threatened, like Banquo's heirs, to 'stretch out to the crack of doom'. I believe they wouldn't have stopped at 50 cards! The rest of the class were most impressed and a

select few were initiated into the rites of play, which the group of boys took very seriously.

King Duncan's Thoughts:

> I thought he was my friend,
> I thought I could trust him.
> He was loyal to me,
> I honoured him.
> I thought I knew him,
> I thought he loved me.
> But I was wrong.

(Pupil aged 9, Newtown Linford Primary)

The Scotsman

The murder

November 1390   2 Groats

OUT DAMNED SPOT.
INTO THE FUTURE.

INTO THE FUTURE

I asked Macbeth what the weird sisters looked like . He gave me a description of them.He said that some had three faces and some had two faces.He said that they could see into the future.He said that they said that he would be KING OF SCOTLAND.But he said that he did not believe them though.He was wrong.So does this mean that there are witches some where out there in Scotland? Can they really see into the future or not? Will you ever see them.

OUT DAMNED SPOT

Macbeth sent for a doctor last night for lady Macbeth.He said she was going mad because she kept saying"Out damned spot,"and rubbing her hands at the same time .So the doctor went up to her to touch her. But she pushed him away from her.She kept saying out damned spot, and rubbing her hands at the same time .Later thatnight Lady Macbeth died. So we will never now why she kept saying out damned spot and rubbing her hands at the same time.

The Caxton Press

Figure 10.1 *Follow-up English/graphics/IT work after seeing Keystage Theatre's production of* Macbeth

Chapter 11

Were the Aims Achieved? An Evaluation

Cherry Stephenson and Peter Walden

The formal evaluation of the Project was undertaken by Peter Walden, the Dean of Education for De Montfort University, supported by members of his staff, in particular Jane Dowson, Elizabeth Grugeon, Joan Stephenson and Roger Stranwick. Cherry Stephenson, the Acting Head of the Leicestershire Drama and Dance Advisory Service, was responsible for liaising with the University team and co-ordinating the evaluation process. *Editor.*

The RSA Shakespeare Project was a co-operative venture between many different agencies who sought to explore what could be done by children and students of all ages from 5 to 18 when they were presented with a play or plays by Shakespeare.

This was from the start a practical exercise, with funding for resources which supported workshops and teaching sessions for the children and students and their teachers. The purposes of those organizing the project are summarized in the Souvenir Programme of the Festival and Exhibition, 9–12 March 1993:

> To have Shakespeare in the classroom or not to have Shakespeare in the classroom, that is the question. John Patten says yes, Michael Bogdanov says no. As they and other cultural leaders shout at each other across the great cultural divide, a family of Leicestershire schools, supported by such eminent institutions as the RSA, the RSC, the Haymarket Theatre and De Montfort University, has, without fuss, explored ways in which children can be introduced to Shakespeare throughout their school life from the age of five to eighteen ... The basis of the project is that Shakespeare, if taught appropriately, can release varied and rich learning experiences for all.
>
> (Maurice Gilmour)

With such diverse participants and sponsors, the Project was many different things to different people, and we have tried in the evaluation to indicate its value to the major categories of participants, as well as its contribution to the teaching of Shakespeare in today's schools.

In order to examine the ways and the extent to which the RSA initiative to 'enrich children's experiences through the "High Arts"' has been achieved during the Shakespeare Project, evidence has been gathered from four sources:

- the children and students
- the participating teachers

- visiting professionals
- teachers not directly involved.

THE AIMS OF THE EVALUATION

The evaluation has endeavoured to:

- establish the aims and purposes of the use of Shakespeare in the participating schools
- analyse the attitudes of individual teachers towards the aims of the Project
- describe methods, strategies and outcomes in a representative sample of schools covering all age ranges from 5 to 18
- analyse approaches and methods used in the Project
- identify wider and longer-term issues related to the teaching of Shakespeare in schools.

MAIN FINDINGS

The evaluation team found an unusually high degree of commitment and co-operation in all participating groups. While teachers from time to time expressed reservations about their heavy workload and low esteem, and emphasized the value of funding to resource in-service training, visiting specialists and teacher cover, there was overwhelming enthusiasm for the opportunities provided by working with Shakespeare's plays in schools.

The specific benefits included:

- the use of Shakespeare as a linguistic and narrative resource
- the enhancement of motivation and morale through giving primary-age children enjoyable experience of working with the plays
- the positive value of performance of different styles and levels to the participants, even when they were young and inexperienced
- the recognition by parents and the wider community of the schools that what was happening was important, generating a common sense of purpose.

The teachers in particular were wary of the problems that Shakespearean texts can present to young people and used ingenious methods to ensure wide participation and enjoyment. To some, the support of additional funding and being part of a recognized project were essential elements in the success of their work. However, there was abundant evidence that confidence, the support of colleagues and clear and positive objectives enabled teachers to develop successful strategies for Shakespeare in the classroom. In fact, many emphasized that successful work of this kind had always been a part of the curriculum of their schools.

STAGES IN THE EVALUATION PROCESS

1. A meeting was held to establish and interpret the aims of the project. It included teachers representing each of the key stages, the project co-ordinator, representatives from the RSA, staff from Leicestershire Drama and Dance Advisory Service and tutors from De Montfort University involved in the Formal Evaluation.
2. Interviews were conducted with teachers on their own response to the aims and their projections for executing them in the classroom.
3. Lessons and workshops were observed, keeping the teachers' aims in mind, followed by interviews with teachers and pupils.
4. The festival and exhibition week provided opportunities to observe performances and displays and note the findings of teachers during the In-Service day.
5. Workshops run by the Royal Shakespeare Company, Haymarket Theatre and Advisory staff were observed with interview follow-up.
6. Written reports produced by teachers and pupils were analysed.
7. Plans were made to follow up a few individual projects in the following year to assess the longer-term effects of the project, through interview and discussion.

AIM OF THE REPORT

At the early meeting with teachers, the aims of the Project were discussed and a strategy developed whereby interviews with teachers would explore the aims and the teachers' response to them with regard to their work with their classes.

The aims and a summary of main findings follow. It should be noted that for the majority of teachers there was a strong emphasis on what they could do in their own classrooms for their children and students. For the teachers, the commitment to their pupils came first, as the people central to the whole Project.

The interviews with teachers were semi-structured, built around a common set of intended outcomes without being a rigid questionnaire. The outcomes were related to the aims of the Project, each teacher being asked of each aim, 'Do you agree with it?' and, 'How do you think it can best be achieved?'

The following is a summary of responses to the question for each aim.

1. **To demonstrate that studying Shakespeare can be an enjoyable activity.** This received universal approval, particularly from teachers of younger children, an attitude which is encouraging from the point of view of the increasing presence of Shakespeare in the National Curriculum. It must be noted, however, that many of the teachers saw the Project as an escape from the constraints of the National Curriculum.
2. **To demonstrate that Shakespeare's plays can be made accessible to students of all abilities from 5–18 years.** The universally approving responses to this are the natural consequence to the support for the first aim,

but teachers were also keen to open up the discussion of how the aim could be achieved. They introduced many exciting ideas, some seeing the text as a starting point and others preferring to start away from the text. The latter were mostly in primary schools, and their starting points varied from improvised drama to visual arts to word games. The wealth of ideas at this level is itself testimony to the value of the Project.

3. **To demonstrate that a variety of approaches are available and have validity.** Again, the aim was approved by all, and there was enthusiasm for the implementation of many of the ideas already introduced by teachers. There was some sense in respect of this question that there were more constraints with the older age groups, whose time was not so readily under the control of the teacher. This feeling showed itself more clearly in the answers to subsequent questions.

4. **To demonstrate that his plays and themes can be used across the curriculum.** Teachers of young children wrestled with this question from the beginning, frequently with great success, and there was no doubt that they were able to introduce topics related to Shakespeare to almost all areas of the curriculum, especially in the arts and humanities. Teachers of older children were much more wary, explaining that the additional communication and liaison necessary to meet this aim in a subject-based curriculum made demands on time and goodwill that many teachers are no longer prepared or able to give. We sympathize with this position. On the other hand, one of the best cross-curricular experiences came from a Year 11 student, who had previously no knowledge of Shakespeare or inclination to find out more. This boy, from a village family and with very little experience beyond his immediate surroundings, worked out a perception of time and change through the language of the plays. We would add that enabling him to do this was an example of teaching of a very high order.

5. **To demonstrate that students can come to an understanding of text both as literature and through performance.** The language of this aim leads to a slightly more formal appraisal of the Project. Teachers were confident that they could lead their classes into the plays both through the text and through performance, and from a very early stage gave many examples of children unexpectedly showing much greater understanding of the text than they would previously have thought possible. They had a variety of views on the importance of access to the text. Those who thought it less important were worried about the use of the Project to convey a 'high culture' message to children at the expense of more pluralist and open approaches to culture and learning. These teachers were in a minority, but the point is well made in that it addresses the definition of a common culture.

6. **To produce resource materials which can be made available to other teachers.** This was the first of the aims which moved away from the classroom, and teachers naturally could not see how they could play more than a part in achieving this aim. Responses varied a little as to its desirability, as some teachers did not want anything to detract from the central business of the education of the children in their classes. Many, though, clearly thought

that they were on to something so good that it ought to be shared with others if at all possible.

7. **To provide collaborative opportunities between schools for different ages.** There was the widest gap here between what was seen as desirable and what was possible. Some teachers were keen to use existing links between schools to further the aim of the Project, but most could not see how it could practically be done within the constraints of time and funding already mentioned. The interviews were of course carried out before the Festival and Exhibition, which provided evidence of excellent collaboration between schools.

8. **To disseminate the evaluation more widely.** Not surprisingly, teachers did not have much of a perception of this, and while they saw the educational aims of the Project as clear, desirable and achievable, it was recognized that sympathetic outside agencies were a necessary means of dissemination.

APPROACHES ADOPTED BY SCHOOLS

This section is included to elaborate on the summarized findings of the teachers. It precedes the discussion of the findings.

The description of what happened in schools is divided into the Key Stages of the National Curriculum:

Key Stage 1:5– 8 years
Key Stage 2:8– 11 years

Key Stage 1

The Reception class and Year 1 and 2 classes in a rural primary school used *Twelfth Night* as a vehicle for exploring storms and feelings of loss. They started with a drama session, with a drama advisory input, which introduced Viola and Sebastian on board a ship in a dreadful storm. The children made the storm using fabric and accompanying the action with sound effects. Then the class discussed in groups how the twins may have felt and how they could be rescued. Out of this came paintings, and boats were built with a variety of materials. Captains' logs were written and voyages planned to many destinations. After several sessions of being afloat, exploring life on board ship and learning the rudiments of water safety, land was sighted. It was Illyria. Here the pupils were introduced to Olivia, Sir Toby Belch and Duke Orsino. This led to castle building and the enactment of royal life with many banquets. The rest of the main story was told and played out and portraits were painted of the key characters. Year 2 pupils also wrote letters to Olivia and Orsino, drew pictures and made models of Olivia in her house.

At another rural primary school the early years were introduced to *A Winter's Tale* through a retelling of the story in which they enacted the storm, the lost sheep and the discovery of the abandoned baby. This was led, as was the subsequent

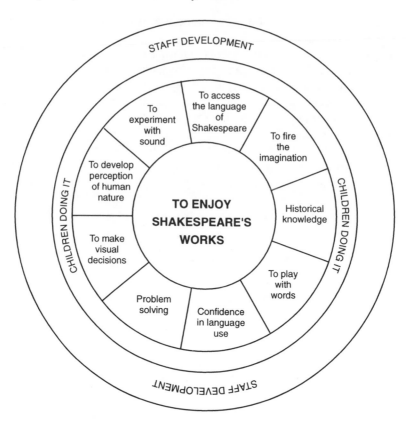

Figure 11.1 *The aims of the RSA Shakespeare Project (Formal evaluation group 14.10.92)*

work, by an advisory teacher, using strategies such as role-playing and framing. The children were engaged in a number of issues, such as what to do about the sheep, the baby's safety and the letter and money they found with the baby.

Years 2 and 3 worked, again with the advisory teacher, on **The Tempest,** looking at the characteristics of Prospero, Ariel and Caliban. The children designed Ariel traps, on the orders of Prospero (teacher in role), and created different aspects of Prospero's island. This provided opportunity for map drawing, learning about terrain, making models and looking at changes in the weather. For instance they looked at the origin of storms from a scientific viewpoint, and also portrayed them in sound and movement and through art work.

Key Stage 2

The two inner-city schools both decided to focus on performance. One, a junior school with 314 pupils, presented a full production of **The Tempest,** lasting two hours and involving over 100 pupils aged between 7 and 11. The Head Teacher

said they were precipitated into this because of a comment made at an early planning meeting of the whole Project that it had to be borne in mind that Shakespeare's text was very difficult for children in their early teens because of the language barrier. This school accepted the challenge and as the Head Teacher put it,
'The language difficulties seemed to evaporate in the action of the play.' He also
comments on how he views the teaching of Shakespeare:

> Opening children's minds to Shakespearean English, such an important and innovative
> component of the language, is a delight and a privilege. For the actors, it was an initia-
> tion, a recognition that the language of Shakespeare is rich, expressive, comic, tender
> and relevant.

The support of the entire staff was enlisted to create a production, with live
music, Renaissance-style costumes, choirs and large dance sequences. The play
was cut and typed out as prose. All the main roles were divided between at least
two performers, to give as many children as possible the opportunity to take a
speaking part, although some roles were not beyond the reach of one child. A section of the play was performed at the Festival and *The Tempest* was performed in
its entirety at school.

A Midsummer Night's Dream was the focus for a rural primary and the other
inner city school. As well as providing a stimulus for art work, science, creative
writing and music, the two schools gave polished but very contrasting performances. The country school presented a twenty-minute version of the whole play in
the children's own words, with a sprinkling of the original script. Led by their class-
teacher, they spent a term exploring different facets of the play, and Shakespeare's
life and times. With an advisory teacher and the class teacher in role as Oberon
and Titania they experienced the warring between the two fairy groups. There
were word games with children learning unfamiliar names and pieces of text.
They designed costumes, made pottery figures, wrote from the point of view of
particular characters, such as Puck's version of the story or how Bottom felt after
the ass's head had been removed. They devised diagrams to show the groupings
and relationships of the play's characters.

The inner-city school, on the other hand, presented the Mechanicals' 'Play
within the play' at the court of the Duke of Athens, with choir and live music,
keeping closely to the script and concentrating on the meaning of the words and
the craft of performance.

King Lear was used by one teacher in a medium-sized rural primary school,
across the curriculum, as a consequence of becoming more and more immersed in
the themes of the play with her class. In addition to the Project's aims, her own
teaching aim was to make Shakespeare relevant to children living in the 1990s.
Through Personal and Social Studies and Religious Education, the mixed-ability
Year 5 and 6 pupils looked at the parent and child relationship and, through im-
provisation, explored Lear's demand for a declaration of love, in a modern context.
They looked at greed and how it affects people's behaviour, the ways that society
treats the elderly, and discussed how the monarchy is regarded in Britain today.
The school had a King Lear day. One pupil was elected to be Lear. He began the
day in full regalia and at lunch-time went first in the dinner queue, but as the day

wore on he was gradually stripped of his royal accoutrements and treated with less and less respect.

The class built up character profiles using the text for clues. The teacher found that they were often very loyal towards the role they had discussed and researched. Even the evil deeds of some of the characters were excused and explained in terms such as 'they had an unhappy childhood', or 'they didn't think they were good at anything' or 'they were looking for attention'.

After working through the play over several weeks the class acted out the main scenes of the story to a parallel class. Planning menus suitable for a Royal feast involved historical research, and calculating the quantities required for Lear and his retinue of 100 followers provided maths work. Sound effects tapes were created to accompany certain scenes and taped interviews were made in the style of television news reports for episodes in the play and also scenes which don't appear. They also looked at Shakespeare the man and the Elizabethan period, which led them into geography, history, science and design technology. These 9–11-year-olds also wrote their own version of Shakespearean language.

THE FESTIVAL AND EXHIBITION

The climax of the two terms of work came with the Festival and Exhibition held in March 1993. There were five elements to this event: an exhibition, workshops by professionals, an in-service day for teachers from participating schools, two evenings of performances by pupils, and a guest evening with a performance of *Macbeth* by Keystage Theatre.

The **exhibition** included a selection of the work produced by each of the participating schools. It featured paintings, pottery, poems, photographs, masks, videos, models, writing and artefacts.

The **workshops** made use of professional support for the Project.

There were four components to the professional input of the Project. These took the form of advisory teacher support from the LEA Drama and Dance Advisory Service, workshops by Wendy Greenhill, the Head of Education of the Royal Shakespeare Company, workshops by the Executive Director, John Blackmore, and Artistic Director, Julia Bardsley, of the Haymarket Theatre, Leicester, and performances of *Macbeth*, directed by Maurice Gilmour and performed by Keystage Theatre, the Theatre in Education company run by Leicestershire Education Committee.

THE IN-SERVICE DAY FOR TEACHERS FROM PARTICIPATING SCHOOLS

The ability to participate in funded in-service activity related to the Project was highly valued by teachers. The day set aside for teachers enabled them to reflect and to share the work covered in different schools during the two terms. Each school had twenty minutes in which to give a presentation on the successes and problems that they and their pupils had experienced in the teaching of Shakespeare.

At this event, as elsewhere, there was evidence of the variety of approaches successfully employed. As suggested in the teacher interviews, primary schools, lacking the constraints of subject timetables, were able to demonstrate that Shakespeare could be taught across the curriculum. It also became apparent that those schools which embarked on production work found that this gave access to technology, science and personal and social education.

At the end of the day, in a letter to colleagues, the teachers said:

- Students' abilities to cope should not be pre-judged.
- Shakespeare explores many issues which even very young children have experienced and in which they can be involved.
- The language, with its sounds, rhythms and meanings, is enjoyed by children – it is an opportunity, not a problem.
- It is best to start with short extracts and focused issues and to leave the full story until later.
- Starting points can equally be a play well known by the teacher or one which is explored alongside students.
- Resources are available and need to be sought out.
- Performance is important, but does not have to be polished.
- Students themselves will make the connections with today's concerns.
- Anyone can understand and enjoy the plays.
- Shakespeare is to be celebrated, not venerated as high art.

Finally, teachers thought that the INSET day, supported by funding for cover, was an essential part of the Project.

THE PERFORMANCES

These were on two evenings, each with a large audience, and consisted of programmes compiled from work by different kinds of schools. The evaluation specifically does not concern itself with the quality of production, although comment will be made below on its role in the teaching of Shakespeare. However, it can be said that the evenings were successful and enjoyable, as reported by teachers, students and the audience.

The Keystage Theatre Performance

Using four actors, Keystage Theatre performed *Macbeth* specially adapted for junior children which retained some of the original text in a performance lasting 55 minutes (Appendix 2). The performance included movement, music and the use of distinctive garments and masks. Shakespearean dialogue was retained, but some connecting narrative provided clarification and continuity.

LEARNING IN THE PROJECT

It would be an impossible task to record in detail the wide range of learning that occurred during the Project. For our purposes evidence will be restricted to activities closely related to the works of Shakespeare, including the area of performance.

It must also be noted that it is not always possible for us to recognize immediately what we have learnt, as this is often a gradual process, so any evaluation of the learning which took place must keep this in mind. The most direct, tangible evidence which was produced took the form of spoken or written statements made by pupils and teachers.

What the children learned in the classroom

It is to be expected that initial responses to the question, 'What have you learned during the Shakespeare Project?' would include bald statements of a factual nature, such as, 'Shakespeare wrote a lot of plays' and 'He lived in Stratford-upon-Avon.' These expanded into comments such as, 'Shakespeare was a very clever man with the sort of books he wrote', 'he is a very talented man' and ''I thought he was only for adults, but now I think he is for all ages' to ' I liked the way all the characters are linked in some way or another. Somehow they are. I also think the way they are all different is very good too.'

Pupils at all ages began to access the meaning of Shakespearean language, whether in role as wordsmiths, lawyers connected with Shylock, attendants to Titania and Oberon or directors of a workshop performance of Richard III. Children certainly found some of the language difficult, obscure and unintelligible, as adults do, but by being given small sections to analyse like detectives, by speaking it aloud, after guidance on the beat and the flow of the words, pupils began to feel that they could unlock the secrets of the text with confidence.

Learning related to performance

Pupils who were involved in performance, recognized that they had developed an understanding of theatre skills, voice projection, timing, symbolism, costuming, developing rapport with the audience. One pupil remarked, 'I learnt to speak loudly so people can hear you', and another commented, 'When you act, you can't just say the words like in a conversation, you have to exaggerate what you do and how you stand, so the audience gets the point. You can't behave normally. In our play of "Pyramus and Thisbe", it has to be sort of slowed down and bigger than normal life.'

There was awareness that considerable time and effort has to go into producing a performance: 'Things take time and as you practise they get better.'

Some primary children demonstrated considerable critical awareness of the whole process of play production from casting to performance. They were able to articulate that the ways they were handled by teachers as actors made them aware of the skills involved in directing. These children noticed how they responded to the encouragement or otherwise of their directors and through this self-awareness they learnt what helped to motivate or stifle the contributions they brought to performance.

Many of the pupils who performed remarked on the social learning which the activity produced. They noticed that they got to know each other better, including children they would normally rarely speak with, and that, of necessity, they had to get on with pupils with whom they wouldn't normally associate. Consequently, children were often surprised to discover that closer proximity with each other often broke down prejudices, leading to an improvement in the social health of the class.

The growth of self-awareness was another learning aspect which students identified during rehearsals, whether grappling with the unfamiliar metre and words which had to be spoken out aloud, working out how best to convey visually what a role was feeling or deciding with others the most effective way to show the interpersonal relationships between characters. Again, primary as well as secondary pupils identified a recognition of the stimulating and marked learning they experienced about their limitations and unexpected strengths through the rehearsal process.

What the teachers learned

Often, what the teachers learned challenged their previous assumptions. This caused them to review their planning. Working on *Twelfth Night* at Key Stage 1, for instance, one teacher wrote, 'I'd expected music and art to come out of the Project (as it did), but there was more of a focus on technology which surprised me. We were a bit tentative at the beginning. We needn't have been. The children absorbed whatever we introduced.'

One teacher was interested to note that it wasn't those children who were most literate who could quickly understand the Shakespearean text, but those who enjoyed role-play situations and could readily identify and empathize with different characters.

Active participation, whether in class or in rehearsal, gave a more immediate perception of the words than a more abstract analysis, which was noted by a performer in *The Tempest*: 'Watching a play, you can't understand it as well as when you are doing it.'

Sometimes the teachers felt that it was their own lack of confidence rather than inhibition on the part of the pupils which prevented them from going more deeply into the language. Several teachers discovered that the children often enjoyed saying the words aloud even when they didn't fully understand the meaning.

Teachers in the primary sector were able to teach Shakespeare across the curriculum more easily than those in secondary schools because of more rigid timetabling and subject specialisms in the latter.

Many teachers found that the animated cartoons were a useful addition to clarifying the general story-line and opened up discussion on interpretation of the text.

There was occasionally an overt reliance on outside expertise which demeaned the teaching skills available within schools. This is not to deny that a specialist can add another dimension, but teachers and their classes establish certain patterns of behaviour and expectation which become difficult to alter, enabling a visitor the advantage of introducing fresh approaches with less resistance.

Sometimes teachers overvalued the visiting specialist while feeling deskilled themselves, not realizing that if they taught the same strategies and given a new class they would achieve similar results. It follows that the best expert support is that which tunes in to the needs of teachers and classes, provides the appropriate learning opportunities and leaves teachers feeling competent and confident to continue to develop the work.

Difficulties

The first problem that teachers observed was, even with a play that you know, how do you get into it? Is there an identifiable series of developmental steps for teachers to use?

The second is the teacher's fear of the language; not being able to give an exact translation of every phrase. This can make teachers vulnerable if they perceive their role to be one of expert and knowledge-giver. This can then inhibit the teacher's desire to introduce the text.

Some teachers felt a lack of confidence in the reading aloud of the text. This was remedied to a degree by the in-service day which Wendy Greenhill ran, but not all teachers could attend. An ideal solution would have been to provide an induction course for all teachers in the Project before they began work with their pupils.

There were often difficulties connected with the normal running of individual schools and also the ever-present pressures of the wider educational picture. It must, in fact, be noted that this project took place despite the considerable changes brought about by government legislation.

Primary teachers felt hampered by their limited specialist knowledge. Sitting down with a play, to read it with understanding and produce palatable teaching material from it, is a time-consuming and demanding task which many teachers found daunting. It suggests that there may be a market, contrary to the opinion of some publishers, for teaching materials at the primary level which support such classroom work in the teaching of Shakespeare.

THE PROJECT AND SHAKESPEARE IN SCHOOLS

The work of the evaluation team was mostly concerned with the participants, with teachers and students and those who supported and visited them.

However, the evaluation would certainly be incomplete if it stepped away from the issues raised about the presence of Shakespeare in schools. In the first place, the very aim of working with all ages and all abilities determined an approach that could not be bound to text. There was, however, a clear imperative to respect the text and to acknowledge its challenges and problems.

The fundamental questions for this part of the evaluation are: 'What value does Shakespeare add to the primary school curriculum?' and 'What approaches and methodologies are best employed to provide this value?'

It is important to keep an eye on these questions related to the experience of Shakespeare because many of the benefits that we saw were serendipitous. There was much excellent drama work, children wrote, painted and sculpted to create excellent displays, and work in language and history had great success.

However, all of these could have happened anyway in well-taught classes, even if without the particular character given them through the Shakespeare Project, and some of the more generalized justifications given by teachers and others do not seem to be sufficient argument in support of the Project. Such qualities as beauty of the language, centrality to heritage and Shakespeare's primacy amongst playwrights do not of themselves present arguments that illuminate what it is that is particular about working in school with Shakespeare.

There is also the problem of potential drawbacks to the introduction of Shakespeare to all ages and all abilities. The spectre of compulsion and of standard stereotyped responses to dully learned texts haunts most adults who have come to enjoy Shakespeare despite their education. Worse still from this point of view, the spectre reappeared during the lifetime of the Project in the form of the new National Curriculum proposals. This last may, of course, have been a positive factor through the heightened consciousness engendered by the national debate.

The other potential drawback was voiced in particular by one of the teachers in the project, who expressed a continuing concern that what was being provided was an experience in high culture, unrelated to the concerns and interests of the majority of people. This worry was brushed aside by many other participants, but needs answering, especially when Shakespeare has most often in the past been for the elite to experience and recent proposals renew anxieties that he might be institutionalized as such into the future.

The task, then, is to assess the value that was added for all, at all stages. The answer would seem to be positive, at least in demonstrating the possibilities. Most teachers answered enthusiastically and most groups of children demonstrated both by their behaviour and by their responses to questions that they were at least fully involved and at best developing abilities and insights that teachers had not thought possible.

The question of how this was achieved begs the question of what precisely the Project was seeking to achieve, given its many and varied aims. There did, however, appear to be specific benefits from the fact that it was the plays and poetry of Shakespeare that were at the heart of the exercise.

The first benefit was one of recognition, especially for younger children. Parents and other adults frequently commented when told that they were doing Shakespeare at school, a fact that is mentioned in several of the interviews with students. The consequent prestige and recognition given to the work was very easily translated into something that was generally seen to be worthwhile.

The second benefit was that the plays of Shakespeare, with their complex narratives, openness to interpretation, challenges to value systems, were genuinely accessible to all ages and abilities. During the Project, not always in production, there were original and thoughtful, if occasionally bizarre, interpretations. Lear, Puck, Ariel, Caliban, were all given new and interesting life as the characters were re-created in performance, text and discussion. There was a genuine finding out of the possibilities of narrative and character, and it was clear that this was made possible by the richness of the text and variety of permissible interpretations. In our sight, no teacher tried to enforce rigid definitions of character: there were no 'right answers' and students were therefore free to engage actively with the plays.

The third benefit was to do with initiation into the culture, but not solely into the 'high culture' where Shakespeare has often been placed so damagingly. If the plays are as accessible as they have proved to be, then they are available to all. They are a national resource and a genuine basis for a shared culture, but the project also proved that they are not to be seen in isolation and that they are open to a variety of approaches and interpretations. Given the successes here, there is no room for passive reading of the text or for rehearsed answers.

Other benefits came directly through the way that the plays were approached. The language was successfully exploited not merely because of its intrinsic quality but because it was approached as a discovery, frequently through work with specific passages, some of them quite short. This produced quotations shouted in the playground and new realizations of meaning. No one would claim that this was universal. There were predictable complaints from older students about difficulty – they could not be patronized by selections or paraphrases – and across quite a range of ages the activities were judged in degrees of 'boring'. However, there were enough positive approaches to the language not to be dismayed by this.

In essence the Project was an exercise in reading in a difficult context. If this is the case, then those who believe that all real reading is a search for meaning won a famous victory. In order to understand, students had to take risks, to guess and to speculate. Sometimes, they were wrong, but they were usually well guided. If they had gone laboriously from word to word from the beginning, they would have been lost.

As an evaluation team, we made it clear that we were reviewing the Project not the quality of performance, but it is important to reflect on the role of the performances within the Project as seen during the Shakespeare Festival. They certainly created a structure, possibly an over-rigid one in that for most the time-scale to the Festival was worryingly short, and they also dictated the styles of working. The effect, though, varied immensely from school to school. Those who were free to spend most time and commitment on the Project were also the schools that produced the most lively and innovative, the least constrained, performances. This, though it was balanced by quite different conclusions from viewing the exhibition, and the findings from the samples of visits to schools were again inconsistent. The exhibitions were of high quality regardless of the approach to the productions, and the work in school often benefited under the constraints of time.

The Festival was crucial to the Project, in that it brought together the participants in celebration and it provided a focus for outsiders as well as participants. It took immense time and energy to mount, and it dominated some of the work. It has been suggested above that the Project was an exercise in reading, and a successful one in that the plays are much better known and understood by a lot of people as a result. The productions were exciting and attracted interest and contributed significantly to this successful reading. The real benefit was seen in the classroom and studio and it may well be that without the spur of performance, this work would not have taken place.

On the evidence of work seen in the Project, the objection to focusing too much and too soon on production is that it closes down meaning and in particular tends to impose the teacher's meaning, in much the same way as being tied to the text in the classroom has done for generations. On the other hand productions explore and experiment with meaning. There were numerous excellent attempts to do this, and the children, given time and the right preparation, worked successfully in terms of their own enjoyment and learning. Without experimentation and discovery, ownership and lasting involvement with the plays would seem to be less likely. However, this process happened to a certain extent in all schools, and with outstanding success in some.

The Project benefits from being set in the context of work with Shakespeare in schools across the country. The enthusiasm, accessibility of the texts and successful classroom work replicate other findings. Fears that without the funding it would not happen are not groundless, but there is every indication from the Project that the most valuable of the experiences for children working with Shakespeare's plays are not heavy on finances or physical resources.

The Project was ambitious and multi-faceted. Its success can be a cornerstone for the presence of Shakespeare in a dynamic and relevant school curriculum.

Chapter 12

An RSA Assessment of the Wider Issues

Penny Egan

The RSA adopted the Shakespeare in Schools Project as a focus for a review of the arts, in particular the 'high arts', within education, at a time when the arts were under threat from new legislation. The RSA took the view that all the arts should be encouraged throughout a pupil's time in school, and that what are deemed the 'high arts' can and should be made accessible to all pupils, whatever their ability. In forming this premise the RSA drew on the Gulbenkian Report of 1982, *The Arts in Schools,* which concluded that the Arts are a necessary component of the curriculum for developing

- the full variety of human intelligence
- the ability for creative thought and action
- the education of feeling and sensibility
- the exploration of values
- understanding of cultural change and differences
- physical and perceptual skills
- vocational training.

The RSA aimed specifically to highlight the value of the arts in the curriculum, to improve access to the arts for all school pupils; to inspire confidence in teachers to deal with a wide spectrum of the arts, including those sometimes thought to be difficult because of historical content or technical or intellectual complexity; to promulgate good practice among head teachers, governors, politicians and policy makers; and to give a focus to the arts at a time when they are under threat from underfunding and weakly represented within the National Curriculum.

In terms of the wider implications of the RSA's involvement, it became clear that the arts were the means through which many pupils became engaged positively in the Shakespeare text. If this seems to be an obvious statement because, after all, his plays were written for the theatre, it has to be said that Shakespeare is not often taught by these methods. Sometimes class work led to performances, but mostly it aimed at achieving a response to the text within the classroom situation. Either way, there is clear evidence that approaches making use of arts processes made the plays accessible to pupils from a very early age and led to increased appreciation and understanding.

The accounts of teachers, the work of the pupils, and the assessment of the evaluation team show that the art forms in themselves were an enriching experience. Comments abound that speak of a marked increase of confidence in speaking and moving, the enjoyment of working as a member of a group, and the growing awareness of the power and characteristics of theatre and art. Those who showed their work through exhibition or performance also gained knowledge about the arts as a different form of communication.

> When the words became overlaid with the ridiculous action, the slapstick, the visual comedy, they began to laugh out loud, and approach the scenes with relish. They always rushed to rehearsal and left wanting to do more.
>
> (Teacher, Coleman Primary)

The point is made in the formal evaluation that many of the benefits perceived by teachers were the results of using arts processes and not necessarily the result of contact with Shakespeare. This is important to note. The whole primary school curriculum can be looked upon as a text , the history of the Tudor period no less than *The Merchant of Venice*. The intricacies of the reformation and the political struggles of the sixteenth century contain within them complexities that are a challenge to any primary teacher. Of course, the history can be delivered in a simplistic manner, but if it is to be meaningful in terms of the children's own lives and lead to their development of knowledge and understanding, they need to be engaged in the material and recognize the links with their own lives: otherwise the figures of history remain shadowy and separate from the forces that govern our lives today. The arts can make this connection. This became all too apparent in the search to make Shakespeare meaningful. The verdict of 80 teachers and 2,000 children acclaimed the success of the search. Not only did they find they were grappling and connecting with a classical writer of world repute, they also found that the arts processes of drama, dance, music and art brought many other benefits and also met attainment targets set down by the National Curriculum.

The Project demonstrated that while some teachers had the necessary skill and confidence, others needed support from colleagues or outside agencies. The benefits derived from professional artists were evident from the work of Key Stage Theatre, the RSC and the Haymarket Theatre. Also, the team of advisory staff from the LEA was of crucial importance in supporting classroom work and co-ordinating the Project. A committed, experienced advisory team can do much for professional and curriculum development.

Following the Shakespeare in Schools Project and the concerns it raised, the RSA in association with the Arts Council of England and the Gulbenkian Foundation commissioned a report in 1994 by Rick Rogers, *Guaranteeing an entitlement to the Arts in schools*. The report recognizes that for the first time there is a legal statement of what a pupil is entitled to in the National Curriculum, and that this must include the expressive arts of art and design, music, dance (through PE) and drama (through English).

But, the report makes clear, the 1988 Education Reform Act has also had an unintentionally detrimental effect on arts education. Two things are happening. There is a growing disparity in the ability of schools to meet the minimum requirements of the National Curriculum. In addition many schools are unable to go beyond that minimum and offer pupils a more wide-ranging and fulfilling experience of the arts. Of particular concern were the figures from a recent Arts Council report, *Looking over the Edge*, which documented the decline of local authority advisory and support services for the arts in schools: the very support that the RSA Shakespeare Project had so heavily relied upon. Of equal concern were the increasing problems that LMS (Local Management of Schools) was presenting for the funding of county-wide provision. Theatre in Education (TIE) groups were finding it hard to find a steady source of income, and many such groups serving education authorities were, the report concluded, increasingly under threat.

The report sets out a series of recommendations that those with influence must urgently address if we are not to further undermine the arts in schools, and put in jeopardy not only our future artists and performers, but also our future audiences.

Those involved in the Project are fully aware of the work in other parts of the country on teaching Shakespeare and the arts in education. However, it is hoped that a project involving a family of schools offers a different perspective and that the conclusions support the view that Shakespeare can and should be made accessible to all and that the arts are an essential part of everyone's education experience.

In particular, the Project found that:

- The study of Shakespeare can be an enriching experience for all pupils aged 5–11 years.
- Shakespeare can be made accessible to all pupils, regardless of ability.
- Teaching approaches should be appropriate to the age and experience of the pupils.
- Performance is a means of exploring text and is valid as a teaching approach.
- Professional theatre performance can inspire curiosity and further study.
- Shakespeare can be a resource for learning in other areas of the curriculum.
- Non-specialist teachers have the necessary skill to make Shakespeare accessible to all their pupils but often lack confidence.

In general, the Project found that:

- Schools are able to give support to their teachers and extend their expertise through sharing their skills in collaborative work.
- Opportunities should be given to teachers from primary and secondary schools to work together.
- Advisory services have a crucial part to play in supporting the professional development of teachers and underpinning collaborative projects.
- Professional artists, through performance or workshops, can make a valuable contribution to the development of the curriculum.
- The arts are a means of approaching many areas of the curriculum.

- In coping with complex Shakespearean text and themes, pupils are making a claim for a revision on the thinking that governs the primary school curriculum.

After taking part in a *Midsummer Night's Dream:*, Mark aged 8, from Thornton Primary School, said 'What're we doing next, Miss? There's a lot to go at.'

Appendix 1

Evaluation of Keystage Theatre's Production of *Macbeth*

Two questionnaires were completed by children from six primary schools in Leicestershire:

Newtown Linford
Stafford Leys
Stanton under Bardon
Thornton
Lady Jane Grey
Markfield Mercenfeld

The questions were devised by a group of staff from the schools and approximately 300 children aged 6–10 years completed the forms. Each questionnaire shows the responses of the children both as one group and in age groups. It is acknowledged that the results can only be used as general indicators since they were in response to one particular production.

LEICESTERSHIRE SHAKESPEARE PROJECT 92/93
KEYSTAGE THEATRE – PRODUCTION OF *MACBETH*

EVALUATION 1

Totals of all schools – individual ages (Lady Jane Grey figures not included as ages were not indicated)

		Response		
Statement	**Age**	**Yes**	**Don't Know**	**No**
1. I was looking forward to seeing the play.	6/7	75	7	4
	8	77	2	1
	9/10	108	16	2
2. I was looking forward to seeing the play because I knew it was a play by Shakespeare	6/7	50	22	14
	8	48	23	9
	9/10	55	47	24
3. The people in Macbeth are like real people.	6/7	39	27	20
	8	39	23	23
	9/10	67	30	29
4. Macbeth's story is a true one.	6/7	30	23	33
	8	22	24	34
	9/10	35	34	57
5. I would like to see more plays by Shakespeare.	6/7	65	8	13
	8	62	10	8
	9/10	103	17	6
6. Shakespeare is only for adults.	6/7	9	6	71
	8	4	10	66
	9/10	5	4	117
7. The play was too long.	6/7	9	6	71
	8	13	9	59
	9/10	11	11	104
8. Shakespeare should be taught in schools.	6/7	42	20	24
	8	59	11	10
	9/10	88	22	16
9. I would like to take part in a play by Shakespeare.	6/7	49	15	22
	8	49	11	20
	9/10	78	20	28
10. I like to watch plays in school.	6/7	76	7	3
	8	78	–	2
	9/10	117	5	4

Totals of all schools – no age bands

Statement	Age	Response		
		Yes	Don't Know	No
1. I was looking forward to seeing the play.	6–10	275	30	12
2. I was looking forward to seeing the play because I knew it was a play by Shakespeare.	6–10	179	96	49
3. The people in Macbeth are like real people.	6–10	154	85	69
4. Macbeth's story is a true one.	6–10	90	97	127
5. I would like to see more plays by Shakespeare.	6–10	250	37	27
6. Shakespeare is only for adults.	6–10	18	20	276
7. The play was too long.	6–10	54	29	231
8. Shakespeare should be taught in schools.	6–10	203	56	55
9. I would like to take part in a play by Shakespeare.	6–10	190	46	73
10. I like to watch plays in school.	6–10	288	16	10

LEICESTERSHIRE SHAKESPEARE PROJECT 92/93
KEYSTAGE THEATRE – PRODUCTION OF *MACBETH*

EVALUATION 2

Totals of all schools – individual ages (Lady Jane Grey figures not included as ages were not indicated)

Statement	Age	Response		
		True	Don't Know	False
1. Macbeth and Banquo were friends.	6/7	55	21	10
	8	64	10	7
	9/10	110	12	4
2. King Duncan made Macbeth Thane of Cawdor.	6/7	66	12	8
	8	60	11	10
	9/10	108	17	1
3. The witches said Banquo would become King of Scotland.	6/7	17	30	39
	8	25	17	39
	9/10	26	8	92
4. Macbeth killed King Duncan with a dagger.	6/7	78	5	3
	8	78	3	–
	9/10	119	8	1
5. King Duncan was killed in Inverness Castle.	6/7	48	30	8
	8	32	34	15
	9/10	50	55	21
6. Malcolm escaped to England.	6/7	61	18	7
	8	65	12	4
	9/10	102	14	10
7. Lady Macbeth saw Banquo's ghost.	6/7	23	16	47
	8	10	6	65
	9/10	27	6	93
8. Lady Macbeth walked in her sleep.	6/7	74	9	3
	8	62	7	12
	9/10	106	10	10
9. Macbeth was killed in battle by Macduff.	6/7	64	18	4
	8	53	23	5
	9/10	100	21	5
10. Macduff was crowned King of Scotland after Macbeth was killed.	6/7	51	17	18
	8	48	12	21
	9/10	50	9	67

Totals of all schools – no age bands

		Response		
Statement	Age	True	Don't Know	False
1. Macbeth and Banquo were friends.	6–10	245	49	22
2. King Duncan made Macbeth Thane of Cawdor.	6–10	255	41	19
3. The witches said Banquo would become King of Scotland.	6–10	76	65	174
4. Macbeth killed King Duncan with a dagger.	6–10	296	15	4
5. King Duncan was killed in Inverness Castle.	6–10	140	130	45
6. Malcolm escaped to England.	6–10	237	55	23
7. Lady Macbeth saw Banquo's ghost.	6–10	78	34	213
8. Lady Macbeth walked in her sleep.	6–10	253	35	27
9. Macbeth was killed in battle by Macduff.	6–10	231	69	15
10. Macduff was crowned King of Scotland after Macbeth was killed.	6–10	160	43	112

Appendix 2

Adapted Script of *Macbeth*

Adapted for primary schools by Keystage Theatre in Education Company for presentation by four actors

Cast

Paul Waring	Macbeth
Ruth Hellier	Lady Macbeth, 2nd witch, Malcolm, murderer, violinist
Jane Perkins	Banquo, Lady Macduff, Hecate, Seyton, doctor
Simon Cuckson	Macduff, Duncan, 1st witch, murderer
Maurice Gilmour	Director

The play is performed in the round with wide aisles in each of the four corners. In each corner there is a small, low stage rostrum that is high enough to sit on and low enough to step on easily. Each rostrum is backed by a stand with an emblem that represents a particular location or group of characters within the play. These are Macbeth's castle, Duncan's castle, the witches' place, and Macduff's Castle combined with England. On the stands hang the costume and artefacts that represent the people in the play. For Macbeth there are his and Lady Macbeth's costumes, the dagger, the doctor's bag and costume, the servant's costume, hoods for the murderers, and the candle-holder. In Duncan's corner are the costumes for Duncan and Malcolm and the crown. Macduff's corner holds the costume for Banquo as well as those for Macduff and Lady Macduff and material to represent the baby. On the stand in the witches' corner hang the two- and three-sided masks. Percussion instruments and the violin are placed strategically in the corners for the actors to play when off-stage or to take onto the stage. The costume stands provide an environment for the play and keep the characters in the audience's mind even though they are not on-stage.

To start the play the four actors, one with violin and three with bodhrans, stand centre stage as a group looking towards the audience. They play a reel and as they do so, they perform a simple dance. It is a fun dance. The aim is to establish that the actors are going to tell a story and that the people and the action are not real but only actors in role. With the violin and one bodhran still playing two actors bring Duncan's heavy cloak and crown to centre stage. A third actor moves centre stage. The music stops suddenly.

Narrator   In another time, the land far to the North known as Scotland, was ruled by a fair King.

The third actor puts on Duncan's cloak and holds the crown over his head. As he puts the crown on, he speaks.

Duncan   His name was Duncan, King of Scotland.

Duncan circles briefly. The reel starts up again as the cloak and crown are returned to Duncan's corner. Three actors bring the costume of Macbeth, Banquo and Macduff onto the stage. The music stops and in the sequence that follows, each of the three actors comes into the centre and puts on a plaid, establishing and announcing their three roles. After each announcement there is a flourish of violin and drum.

Narrator   Scotland is at war, and leading the fight against the enemy are
three
              brave lords.
Banquo   Cousin of the King – Banquo.

Flourish of violin and bodhrans.

Macduff   The Thane of Fife, Macduff.

Flourish of violin and bodhrans.

Macbeth   The Thane of Glamis, Macbeth.

Flourish of violin and bodhrans. The three make still image centre stage.

Narrator   And in the final battle, the three friends fight side by side at the head of the Scottish army.

There follows a representation of the battle with the three Scots making a range of patterned movements – advancing in line, defending each other etc. – completed by still images. The bodhrans are used as shields and beaten as drums to give the sound of war. The fourth actor plays percussion in a corner to add to the sound of battle. There is a final still image depicting victory.

Narrator   Victory! The war is over and Scotland is safe.

They unfreeze. They part in mime as friends. Macduff goes to one corner, and Macbeth and Banquo to another. They freeze.

Narrator   Macduff rides ahead to announce the famous victory throughout
                  Scotland. Banquo and Macbeth head towards the King, but on the
                  way have an encounter that will change their lives.

An actor comes back on stage in basic, carrying a mask. He shows the mask to the audience. He is joined by a second actor, also carrying a mask. They face each other.

1st Actor   Some call them magicians, some call them prophets, some call
                  them fortune tellers, but we call them –

They put the masks on slowly.

Both   – the weird sisters!

The first witch leaps onto one of the rostra and sings in a childish way, pointing to the second witch.

1st Witch   I'm the King of the Castle, and you're the dirty rascal.

The second witch comes towards him playing the tune on the violin in an increasingly threatening manner. She plays and sings and forces the first witch from the rostrum and onto his knees. The game has become unpleasant. It's as if the violin were a weapon.

2nd Witch   I'm the King of the Castle, and you're the dirty rascal.

Suddenly they are both aware of something in the air. The second witch plays a discordant sequence of notes on the violin. The first witch plays the bodhran quietly.

Both   Fair is foul and foul is fair,
                  Hover through the fog and filthy air.

Macbeth and Banquo make a distant marching sound on their bodhrans.

Both   A drum, a drum, Macbeth doth come.

Macbeth and Banquo halt when they see the witches.

1st Witch   All hail, Macbeth.
2nd Witch   Hail to thee, Thane of Glamis.
                  All hail Macbeth.
1st Witch   Hail to thee, Thane of Cawdor.
Macbeth   Cawdor?
                  I know I am Thane of Glamis
                  But how of Cawdor? The Thane of Cawdor lives,

	A prosperous gentleman. Tell me more.
1st Witch	All hail Macbeth.
2nd Witch	That shalt be King hereafter.
Macbeth	To be King stands not within the prospect of belief
	No more than to be Thane of Cawdor.
Banquo	Good sir, why do you start and seem to fear
	Things that do sound so fair? In the name of truth
	Are ye fantastical, or that indeed
	Which outwardly ye show?
	If you can look into the seed of Time
	And say which grain will grow and which will not
	Speak then to me, who neither beg, nor fear
	Your favours, nor your hate.
1st Witch	Hail.
2nd Witch	Hail.
1st Witch	Hail.
	Lesser than Macbeth.
2nd Witch	And greater.
1st Witch	Not so happy.
2nd Witch	Yet much happier.
1st Witch	Your sons shall be king,
2nd Witch	Though thou be none.
1st Witch	So all hail Macbeth and Banquo,
2nd Witch	Banquo and Macbeth, all hail.

The actors take off the masks and the witches have effectively disappeared.

Banquo	The earth hath bubbles, as the water has,
	And these are of them: whither are they vanish'd?
Macbeth	Into the air: and what seem'd corporal,
	Melted, as breath into the wind.
	Would they had stay'd.
	Your children shall be kings.
Banquo	You shall be King.
Macbeth	And Thane of Cawdor too: went it not so?
Banquo	To the selfsame tune and words.

Macbeth and Banquo beat out strong processional sound on the bodhrans as actors come onto the stage with the costumes of Duncan and Malcolm. Duncan puts on cloak as drumming stops and the crown after saying who he is. Malcolm does likewise. Macbeth and Banquo kneel.

Duncan	King Duncan, and his son Malcolm, stood before Macbeth and
Banquo	at the head of the victorious Scottish army.
Mac/Ban	Hail to our royal Master, hail King of Scotland.
Duncan	Macbeth ...
	Brave Macbeth, well do you deserve that name.

>The Thane of Cawdor lives yet,
>But under heavy judgement bears that life
>Which he deserves to lose.
>Treasons capital, confessed and proved
>Have overthrown him.
>What Cawdor hath lost
>Noble Macbeth hath won.

Macbeth goes to the King who puts the Cawdor medallion round his neck as a mark of his new honour. Banquo drums as a background to the ceremony. Everyone freezes in a still image except Macbeth.

Macbeth   Hail to thee Thane of Cawdor.
              Hail to thee, King that shalt be.
              Why, if chance will have me King,
              Why, chance may crown me without my stir.

Everyone unfreezes, and it is at this point that the King puts the medallion round Macbeth's neck.

Duncan   What Cawdor hath lost,
              Noble Macbeth hath won.
              Noble Banquo,
              Let me enfold thee and hold thee to my heart.
              Son, kinsmen, thanes,
              We will establish our estate upon
              Our eldest Malcolm whom we name hereafter,
              The Prince of Cumberland.

Malcolm comes to the King who takes off his own crown and in ceremonial fashion holds it over Malcolm's head. They all freeze except for Macbeth.

Macbeth   The Prince of Cumberland; that is a step
              On which I must fall down, or else o'erleap,
              For in my way it lies.

Macbeth kneels again and as he does so everyone unfreezes.

Duncan   From hence to Dunsinane
              And bind us further to you.
Macbeth   I'll make joyful the hearing of my wife with your approach;
              So humbly take my leave.
Duncan   My worthy Cawdor.

Duncan and Malcolm exit. Macbeth and Banquo are left alone.

Macbeth   Do you not hope your children shall be kings

	When those that gave Thane of Cawdor to me,
	Promis'd no less to them?
Banquo	'Tis strange
	That oftentimes, to win us to our harm,
	The instruments of darkness tell us truths;
	Win us with honest trifles, to betray's
	In deepest consequence.

Banquo exits.

Macbeth	Stars hide your fires,
	Let not light see my black and deep desires.

Macbeth exits as the actor playing Lady Macbeth enters carrying her costume. She puts it on as she speaks.

Narrator	Lady Macbeth, wife of Macbeth, waited in Dunsinane Castle for the return of her husband. As she waited, she read and re-read the letter that Macbeth had sent.

Lady Macbeth reads the letter aloud to herself. Sometimes it is Macbeth's voice we hear and not hers. She has an actual letter in her hand.

LMacbeth	'They met me in the day of success; and I have learn'd by the perfect'st report, they have more in them than mortal knowledge. When I burnt in desire to question them further, they made them selves air, into which they vanish'd. Whiles I stood rapt in the wonder of it, came missives from the King, who all-hailed me Thane of Cawdor, by which title before these Weird Sisters saluted me, and referr'd me to the coming on of time, with hail King that shalt be. Thishave I thought good to deliver thee (my dearest partner of greatness) that thou mightst not lose the dues of rejoicing by being ignorant of what greatness is promis'd thee. Lay it tothy heart and farewell.'

Macbeth has entered towards the end of the reading of the letter. He and his wife embrace and show their closeness.

LMacbeth	Glamis thou art, and Cawdor, and shalt be
	What thou art promised: hail king that shalt be.
	Yet I do fear thy nature;
	It is too full o'th'milk of human kindness.
Macbeth	My dearest love,
	Duncan comes here tonight.
LMacbeth	And when goes hence?
Macbeth	Tomorrow – as he purposes.
LMacbeth	O never

Shall sun that morrow see.
The King comes here tonight.
The raven himself is hoarse
That croaks the fatal entrance of King Duncan
Under my battlements. Come you spirits,
And fill me from the crown to the toe, top-full
Of direst cruelty.
Your face, my thane, is as a book where men
May read strange matters: bear welcome in your eye,
Your hand, your tongue: look like th'innocent flower
But be the serpent under't. King Duncan
Must be provided for; and you shall put
This night's great business into my despatch
Which shall to all our nights and days to come
Give solely sovereign sway and masterdom.

Macbeth	We will speak further.
LMacbeth	Only look up clear:
	To alter favour, ever is to fear:
	Leave all the rest to me.

Lady Macbeth ushers Macbeth away and turns to welcome Duncan and Banquo.

Duncan	Our honoured hostess.
LMacbeth	Welcome my honoured lord.
Duncan	This castle hath a pleasant seat; the air
	Nimbly and sweetly recommends itself
	Unto our gentle senses.
	Fair and noble hostess. We are your guest tonight.
LMacbeth	All our service were poor
	Against those honours deep, and broad,
	Wherewith your Majesty loads our House.
Duncan	Conduct me to mine host. We love him highly.

Everyone freezes. Macbeth enters. He has a dagger in his hand and goes towards the King.

Macbeth	If it were done, when 'tis done, then 'twere well
	It were done quickly. But in these cases
	We still have judgement here, and even-handed Justice
	Commends th'ingredients of our poisoned chalice
	To our own lips. He's here in double trust;
	First, as I am his cousin, and his subject,
	Strong both against the deed; then as his host
	Who should against his murderer shut the door,
	Not bear the knife myself.

Macbeth pulls Lady Macbeth from the still image. Duncan and Banquo form another still image as if talking.

Macbeth	We will proceed no further in this business:
	He hath honoured me of late.
LMacbeth	Art thou afear'd? And wouldst thou
	Live a coward in thine own esteem?
	Letting I dare not, wait upon I would.
	From this time, such I account your love.
Macbeth	I dare do all that may become a man.
	Who dares do more, is none.
LMacbeth	When you durst do it, then you were a man.
	I know how tender 'tis to love a baby, but
	I would, while it was smiling in my face
	Dashed its brains out, had I so sworn
	As you have done to this.
Macbeth	If we should fail?
LMacbeth	We fail?
	But screw your courage to the sticking place,
	And we'll not fail; when Duncan is asleep
	His two chamberlains
	Will I with wine, and wassail so convince
	That memory, the warder of the brain
	Shall be a fume: when in swinish sleep
	Their drenched natures lie as in a death,
	What cannot you and I perform upon
	Th'unguarded Duncan? What not put upon
	The chamberlains who shall bear the guilt
	Of our great quell.
Macbeth	Will it not be received
	When we have mark'd with blood those sleepy two
	Of his own chamber, and us'd their very daggers,
	That they have done't?
LMacbeth	Who dares receive it other?
Macbeth	I am settled.
	Away, and mock the time with fairest show,
	False face must hide what the false heart doth know.

Duncan and Banquo unfreeze. Lady Macbeth, smiling, goes towards the King.

L Macbeth	Goodnight my liege.
Duncan	Goodnight honoured hostess.
Banquo	Goodnight my lord.
Duncan	Goodnight Banquo.

Lady Macbeth and Banquo exit. The actor playing the King takes off the cloak and crown. He lays them on the floor as if they are the sleeping King. He speaks as he looks down at the sleeping form.

Narrator   King Duncan sleeps, protected by his two chamberlains, and safe
               in the castle of his loyal subject, Macbeth. It is very dark, and
               Banquo cannot sleep.

Banquo patrols restlessly. Macbeth enters and edges towards the King. Banquo senses there is someone there.

Banquo   Who's there? ... who's there?
Macbeth   A friend.
Banquo   What sire, not yet at rest? The King's a-bed.
               I dreamt last night of the three weird sisters.
               To you they have showed some truth.
Macbeth   I think not of them.
               Yet, when we can entreat an hour to serve,
               We would spend it in some words upon that business
               If you would grant the time.
Banquo   At your kind'st leisure.
Macbeth   If you shall cleave to my consent when 'tis,
               It shall make honour for you.
Banquo   So I lose none
               In seeking to augment it, but still keep
               My bosom franchised and allegiance clear,
               I shall be counselled.
Macbeth   Good repose the while.
Banquo   Thanks sir; the like to you.

Banquo starts to exit but hesitates. He senses something amiss.

Macbeth   Good repose.

Banquo finally goes. Macbeth draws a dagger and approaches the King. He baulks at the act of murder and backs off, sheathing the dagger. At that moment there is a sound of a violin note and Hecate appears with a dagger. The dagger moves around in space, followed by Macbeth and a haunting note on the violin. The dagger seems to hypnotize him and he is drawn towards it.

Macbeth   Is this a dagger which I see before me,
               The handle towards my hand? Come, let me clutch thee.
               I have thee not, and yet I see thee still.
               Art thou but a dagger of the mind, a false creation,
               In form as palpable
               As this which now I draw.
               Thou marshall'st me the way that I was going,

And such an instrument I was to use.

The dagger is like a magnet drawing Macbeth towards the King. It then hovers over the sleeping body. It is clear then that Macbeth is going to murder the King. The witch and the dagger disappear. The violin stops.

Macbeth   Whiles I threat, he lives.

There is the sound of a bell played on a cymbal.

> I go, and it is done: the bell invites me.
> Hear it not, Duncan, for it is a knell
> That summons thee to heaven or to hell.

Macbeth symbolically murders Duncan by stabbing the King's cloak. It is done slowly with the violin echoing the jarring, tortured act. There is a silence. Suddenly a voice is heard, as if calling out in sleep.

Macbeth   Who's there?

Lady Macbeth enters.

LMacbeth   Alack, I am afraid they have awak'd
             And 'tis not done: had he not resembled
             My father has he slept, I had done't.

Macbeth stumbles from the King's bedchamber and meets Lady Macbeth.

Macbeth   I have done the deed:
             Didst thou not hear a noise?
LMacbeth   I heard the owl scream and the crickets cry.
             Did not you speak?
Macbeth   When?
LMacbeth   Now.
Macbeth   As I descended?
LMacbeth   Ay.
Macbeth   Hark, who lies i'th'second chamber?
LMacbeth   Malcolm.
Macbeth   This is a sorry sight.
LMacbeth   A foolish thought to say a sorry sight.
Macbeth   I thought I heard a voice cry Sleep no more;
             Macbeth does murder sleep, the innocent Sleep,
             Sleep that knits up the ravell'd sleave of care.
LMacbeth   What do you mean?
Macbeth   Still it cried, Sleep no more to all the House:
             Cawdor hath murdered sleep; Macbeth shall sleep no more.
LMacbeth   Go get some water,

	And wash this filthy witness from your hand.
	Why did you bring these daggers from the place?
	They must lie there: go carry them, and smear
	The sleepy grooms with blood.
Macbeth	I'll go no more:
	I am afraid to think what I have done.
	Look on't again I dare not.
LMacbeth	Give me the daggers. If he do bleed,
	I'll gild the faces of the chamberlains,
	for it must seem their guilt.

Lady Macbeth takes the daggers from her husband and carries them to the chamberlains' room. She comes back, her hands covered in blood. Suddenly there is a knocking sound at the door.

Macbeth	Whence is that knocking?
	Will all great Neptune's Ocean wash this blood
	Clean from my hand?
LMacbeth	My hands are of your colour: but I shame
	To wear a heart so white.

More knocking.

	I hear a knocking at the south entry;
	A little water clears us of this deed.
Macbeth	To know my deed –

More knocking.

	'Twere best not know myself.
	Wake Duncan with thy knocking;
	I would thou couldst.

Macbeth exits, followed by Lady Macbeth. The knocking ceases. The actor playing Macduff enters carrying the Macduff costume. He speaks as narrator.

| Narrator | The long night passed. With morning came Macduff, the Thane of Fife, to wake the King. |

The actor puts on Macduff's costume as if it were morning. Macduff approaches the King's bedchamber and calls from outside. When he receives no answer from the King, he looks inside and sees that the King has been murdered. He goes out of the chamber and sounds the alarm and then returns to the side of the King.

| Macduff | O horror, horror, horror. |
| | Ring the alarum-bell: murder and treason, |

Banquo and Donalbain: Malcolm awake,
Shake off this downy sleep, Death's counterfeit,
And look on Death itself: up, and see
The great doom's image.

Gradually there is the sound of bells and drums. Macbeth, Lady Macbeth and Banquo appear. They show bewilderment. Macduff comes out of the King's bed-chamber, carrying the body of Duncan. Macbeth rushes into the Chamberlains' room.

Macduff	O Banquo, Banquo, our royal master's murdered.
LMacbeth	What in our house?
Banquo	Too cruel anywhere. By whom?
Macduff	Those of his chamber, as it seem'd had done't;
	Their hands and faces were all badg'd with blood,
	So were their daggers.
	No man's life was to be trusted with them.

Macbeth comes out of the groom's bedchamber.

Macbeth	Oh yet I do repent me of my fury,
	That I did kill them.

There is a moment of shocked silence.

Macduff	Wherefore did you so?
Macbeth	Here lay Duncan,
	His silver skin laced with his golden blood,
	There the murderers,
	Steeped in the colours of their trade, their daggers
	Unmannerly breeched with gore. Who could refrain,
	That had a heart to love and in that heart
	Courage to make's love known?

Lady Macbeth exits. Macduff and Banquo lay the dead King on the ground. Macbeth gives the crown to Banquo who puts it at the head of the body. They all kneel.

Banquo	Let us meet
	And question this most terrible piece of work
	To know it further.

The three men make a pact. They go to exit. Malcolm enters. The three watch him. Malcolm goes to the body and kneels. He looks up at Macduff.

Macduff	Malcolm, your royal father's murdered.
Malcolm	O, by whom?

Macduff   Those of his chamber, as it seemed, had done't.

Malcolm grieves over his father. Macduff and Banquo turn away and freeze. Macbeth, smiling, continues to look towards Malcolm.

Malcolm   There's daggers in men's smiles
               And our safest way
               Is to avoid the aim. I'll to England.

Malcolm takes up the crown. He kisses it. It is like a farewell. Macbeth comes up to him and takes the crown. Malcolm exits. The bodhrans are beaten as a procession carries off the King's body. The drumming continues as Macbeth is crowned king by Banquo and Macduff. Banquo and Macduff exit leaving Macbeth and his wife as the new King and Queen. Macbeth teases Lady Macbeth with the crown and then puts it on her head. They embrace, laughing. Lady Macbeth walks around feeling the weight and importance of the crown. She sits on the throne – Queen of Scotland. Macbeth comes to her. He bends down to kiss her. As he does so, he snatches the crown from her head and puts it on his own. He smiles but stares at her until she leaves the throne and he sits down. There is suddenly uncertainty in her manner. She sits behind him. Quick drumming heralds Banquo's entrance. It is clear that the relationship between Macbeth and Banquo has now changed. Banquo stands in front of Macbeth, who regards him with an unsmiling face.

Banquo   You asked for me, my liege.
Macbeth   Tonight we hold a solemn supper sir,
               And I'll request your presence.
Banquo   Let your Highness command upon me.
LMacbeth   Fail not our feast.
Banquo   My lady, I will not.
Macbeth   We hear our cousin Malcolm is bestow'd
               In England.
Banquo   Ay my good Lord; our time does call upon's.
Macbeth   Farewell.

   Banquo freezes as he exits.

Macbeth   To be thus is nothing, but to be safely thus.
               Our fears in Banquo stick deep,
               He hath a wisdom, that doth guide his valour
               To act in safety. There is none but he
               Whose being I do fear. He chid the Sisters
               When first they put the name of King upon me,
               And bad them speak to him. Then prophet-like,
               They hail'd him father to a line of Kings.
               Upon my head they plac'd a fruitless crown.
               For Banquo's sons have I fil'd my mind,

	For them the gracious Duncan have I murdered.
LMacbeth	What's done is done.
Macbeth	We have scorch'd the snake, not kill'd it.
LMacbeth	You must leave this.
Macbeth	O full of scorpions is my mind, dear wife;
	Thou know'st that Banquo and his son live.
LMacbeth	My lord, you must leave this.
Macbeth	There's comfort yet, they are assailable.

A murderer enters. Lady Macbeth looks at him in alarm.

LMacbeth	What's to be done?
Macbeth	Be innocent of the knowledge, dearest chuck,
	Till thou applaud the deed: but hold thee still,
	Things bad begun, make strong themselves by ill.

Lady Macbeth registers that her husband is now following his own track. She exits. Macbeth nods towards the murderer and hands over a pouch of money.

It is concluded. Banquo, thy soul's flight,
If it find heaven, must find it out to-night.

Banquo unfreezes as he is approached by the murderer. The killing is done in slow motion. The murderer covers Banquo in a net. He then uses a scraper to indicate by sound the act of killing. Banquo lies where he has been killed and the murderer exits. Lady Macbeth enters. It is the feast.

LMacbeth	Gentle my lord, sleek o'er your rugged looks.
Macbeth	Duncan is in his grave; he sleeps well.
	Treason has done his worst, nor steel nor poison
	Can touch him further.
LMacbeth	Be bright and jovial among your guests to-night.
Macbeth	So shall I, love, and so I pray be you.

Macduff enters.

Macduff	Your majesties.
LMacbeth	A hearty welcome.
Macduff	Thanks to your majesty.
LMacbeth	My royal lord
	You do not give the cheer.
Macbeth	Sweet remembrancer;
	Now good digestion wait on appetite
	And health on both.
	Here had we now our country's honour roof'd
	Were the grac'd person of our Banquo present:

Macduff His absence, sir
      Lays blame upon his promise.

*They freeze. Banquo's ghost rises, the net pulled tight over the head. All the
actors make a breathing sound. The ghost sits on the throne. They all unfreeze.*

Macduff May't please your Highness sit.

Macbeth sees the ghost on the throne.

Macduff What is't that moves your Highness?
Macbeth Which of you have done this?
Macduff What my good lord?
Macbeth Thou canst not say I did it: never shake
      Thy gory locks at me.
Macduff His Highness is not well.
LMacbeth My Lord is often thus and hath been from his youth.
      Are you a man?
Macbeth Ay and a bold one that dare look on that
      Which might appal the Devil.
LMacbeth This is the very painting of your fear:
      This is the air-drawn dagger which you said
      Led you to Duncan; shame itself,
      Why do you make such faces?
Macbeth Prithee see there.
      Behold, look, lo, how say you?
      Why what care I, if thou canst nod, speak too.

They freeze. The ghost exits to the same breathing sound. They unfreeze.

      The time has been
      That, when the brains were out, the man would die,
      And there an end. But now they rise again.
LMacbeth My worthy lord,
      Your noble friend doth lack you.
Macbeth I do forget.
      Do not muse at me my most worthy friend,
      I have a strange infirmity which is nothing
      To those that know me. Come, love and health to all
      And to our dear friend Banquo, whom we miss.
      Would he were here.
Macduff Our duties and the pledge.

The ghost enters, accusing Macbeth.

Macbeth Avaunt and quiet my sight, let the earth hide thee:
      Thy bones are marrowless, thy blood is cold.

LMacbeth	Think of this good peers
	But as a thing of custom: 'tis no other,
	Only it spoils the pleasure of the time.
Macbeth	Take any shape but that, and my firm nerves
	Shall never tremble. Hence, horrible shadow.
	Unreal mockery, hence.

The ghost of Banquo exits.

LMacbeth	You have displac'd the mirth,
	Broke the good meeting, with most admir'd disorder.
Macbeth	You can behold such sights
	And keep the natural ruby of your cheeks,
	When mine is blanch'd with fear?
Macduff	What sights my lord?
LMacbeth	I pray you speak not: he grows worse and worse:
	Question enrages him: at once, good night.
Macduff	Good night and better health attend his majesty.
LMacbeth	A kind goodnight to all.

Macduff exits.

Macbeth	It will have blood they say:
	Blood will have blood.
	Stones have been known to move, and trees to speak:
	I will tomorrow to the Weird Sisters.
	More shall they speak.
	Strange things I have in head.
LMacbeth	You lack the season of all natures, sleep.
Macbeth	Come we'll to sleep.
	We are yet but young in deed.

Macbeth and Lady Macbeth exit. Witch enters wearing mask. Sees crown on throne. Puts it on and crouches on the throne. Sings 'I'm the King of the Castle' song twice – once with each of the faces on the mask. Witch enters with violin. Dances round throne as witch sings. Accompanies singing on violin.
   Violin also plays for the charm.

Both	Double double toil and trouble
	Fire burn and cauldron bubble.

The crown is treated like a cauldron. They then circle each other on the floor accompanying their chanting with violin and bodhran.

Both	Fillet of fenny snake,
	In th' cauldron boil and bake:
	Eye of newt, and toe of frog,

Wool of bat and tongue of dog:
Adder's fork, and blind-worm's sting,
Lizard's leg, and howlet's wing:
For a charm of powerful trouble,
Like a hell-broth, boil and bubble.
Round about the cauldron go
In the poisoned entrails throw.
Toad, that under cold stone.
Days and nights, has thirty one;
Swelter'd venom sleeping got,
Boil thou first i' th' charmed pot.

Hecate enters. She seizes the crown and stands on the throne.

Hecate   I'm King of the Castle.

The witches dance round Hecate. The violin and bodhran play as they chant.

Witches   Double double toil and trouble;
              Fire burn, and cauldron bubble.
              Round about the cauldron go
              In the poisoned entrails throw.
              Toad, that under cold stone,
              Days and nights, has thirty one;
              Swelter'd venom sleeping got,
              Boil thou first i' th' charmed pot.
Witch   By the pricking of my thumbs –

The witch is interrupted by Hecate.

Hecate   By the pricking of my thumbs,
              Something wicked this way comes.
All   Open locks, whoever knocks.

Macbeth enters. The witches try to hide the crown. Childlike they try to play a game with him. He is very adult and angry and finally grabs the crown from them.

Macbeth   What is't you do?
W1   Macbeth
W2   Macbeth
W3   Macbeth
All   Beware Macduff,
              Beware the Thane of Fife, dismiss me. Enough.
W1   Macbeth
W2   Macbeth
W3   Macbeth
All   Macbeth shall never vanquished be, until

	Great Birnam Wood to high Dunsinane Hill
	Shall come against him.
Macbeth	That will never be:
	Who can impress the forest, bid the tree
	Unfix his earth-bound root?
All	Macbeth shall never vanquished be, until
	Great Birnam Wood to high Dunsinane Hill
	Shall come against him.
Macbeth	That will never be.
All	Show his eyes, and grieve his heart,
	Come like shadows, so depart.

The witches remove their masks. By doing so, they disappear.

Macbeth	Infected be the air whereon they ride
	And damn'd all those that trust them.

Macbeth watches as Lady Macduff enters carrying a baby. She is singing a gentle song accompanied by the violin. Macduff enters. He and his wife embrace. They freeze.

Macbeth	Macduff is fled to England.
	The Castle of Macduff I will surprise,
	Seize upon Fife: give to th'edge o' th' sword
	His wife, his babes.

Macduff and Lady Macduff unfreeze. In mime, he says farewell and as he exits he turns and they wave to each other. Macduff exits. Lady Macduff freezes. A murderer comes to Macbeth.

Macbeth	Give to th'edge of the sword
	His wife, his babes.

The murderer, armed with a scraper, moves slowly towards Lady Macduff as she slowly unfreezes. Lady Macduff and her child are killed. The murderer exits. Macduff enters, picks up the dead baby, and kneels by his wife's body. the actors off-stage speak to him.

Off Stage	Your castle is surprised, your wife and babes
	Savagely slaughtered.
Macduff	My children too?
All	Wife, children, servants, all
	That could be found.
Macduff	Macbeth.
	Macbeth has no children.
	All my pretty ones. At one fell swoop.
	Did heaven look on and would not take their part?

Heaven rest them now.
*The violin plays the air that established Lady Macduff when she first ap-
peared. As it plays, Lady Macduff slowly rises, takes the baby and slowly exits,
not looking at her husband. The violin stops.*

Macduff	Be this the whetstone of my sword;
	Within my sword's length set him.
	Dunsinane castle he strongly fortifies.
	Some say he's mad.
	Now does he feel
	His secret murders sticking on his hands;
	Now does he feel his title
	Hang loose upon him like a giant's robe
	Upon a dwarfish thief.
	Our power is ready. Macbeth is ripe for shaking
	Now we'll march with ten thousand warlike men
	Towards Birnam Wood and on to Dunsinane.

*Macduff exits. A doctor enters and goes to Macbeth who makes a sign to keep
silent. Lady Macbeth enters. She carries a candle holder and lighted candle. she
is sleep-walking. During the ensuing scene, in the middle of a line of thought, she
suddenly stops and is still as if in a deep trance or asleep on her feet. On these
occasions the doctor examines her close to and is startled by Lady Macbeth suddenly moving and speaking. As she comes in, Lady Macbeth sings an eerie tune to
the words, 'The Thane of Fife, had a wife'. She repeats the melody occasionally
throughout the scene.*

Macbeth	Lo you, here she comes; this is her very guise and upon my life fast sleep; observe her, stand close.
Dr	How came she by that light?
Macbeth	Why it stood by her; she has light by her continually, 'tis her command.
LMacbeth	Yet, here's a spot. Out damned spot: out I say. One two; why then 'tis time to do't. Hell is murky. Fie, my Lord, fie, a soldier and afear'd? What need we fear? Who knows it, when none can call our power to accompt: yet who would have thought the old man to have had so much blood in him.
Dr	Do you mark that?
LMacbeth	The Thane of Fife had a wife: where is she now? What will these hands ne'er be clean? No more o'that my Lord, no more o'that; you mar all this with your starting. Here's the smell of the blood still. All the perfumes of Arabia will not sweeten this little hand. Oh, oh, oh.
Dr	I would not have such a heart for the dignity of the whole body. This
This	disease is beyond my practice.
LMacbeth	Wash your hands, look not so pale; I tell you yet again Banquo's buried; he cannot come out on's grave. To bed, to bed: there's

	knocking at the gate. Come, come, come, come, give me your hand; what's done, cannot be undone. To bed, to bed, to bed.
Dr	She is troubled with thick-coming fancies that keep her from her rest.
Macbeth	Cure her of that. Canst thou not minster to a mind diseased, pluck from the memory a rooted sorrow?
Dr	Therein the patient must minister to himself.

Lady Macbeth exits followed by the doctor. She leaves the light on the throne where she put it when she first came in. Macbeth kneels before the throne. He takes out his dagger and prepares to commit suicide as he speaks.

Macbeth	I am sick at heart.
	I have lived long enough.
	That which should accompany old age,
	As honour, love, obedience, troops of friends,
	I must not look to have; but in their stead,
	Curses, not loud, but deep.

Before he commits the act there is a scream off-stage followed by a mournful bell sound and keening. Macbeth rises. The doctor enters.

Dr	Lady Macbeth, the queen, my lord is dead.
Macbeth	She should have died hereafter.
	There would have been a time for such a word –

The doctor exits.

Tomorrow, and tomorrow, and tomorrow,
Creeps in this petty pace from day to day,
To the last syllable of recorded time;
And all our yesterdays have lighted fools
The way to dusty death.

Macbeth blows out the candle.

Out, out brief candle.
Life's but a walking shadow, a poor player,
That struts and frets his hour upon the stage
And then is heard no more. It is a tale
Told by an idiot, full of sound and fury,
Signifying nothing.

There is a sound of military drumming. Enter Hecate as a servant.

| Hecate | There is ten thousand soldiers sir. |
| Macbeth | What soldiers, patch? What soldiers whey-face? |

Hecate	The English force.
Macbeth	Give me my armour.
	Hang those that talk of fear.
	I'll fight till from my bones my flesh be hacked.
	I will not be afraid of death and bane
	Till Birnam forest come to Dunsinane.

Macbeth and servant exit. Drumming. Enter Malcolm and Macduff and the English army.

Malcolm	What wood is this before us?
Macduff	The wood of Birnam,
Malcolm	Let every soldier hew him down a bough
	And bear't before him.
Macduff	It shall be done.

Drumming. Macduff brings leafy branches onto stage. Malcolm takes one.

Malcolm	We learn no other, but the confident Tyrant
	Keeps still in Dunsinane, and will endure
	Our setting down before it.
Macduff	It is his main hope.
Malcolm	Advance the war.

Malcolm and Macduff conceal themselves behind the branches. Macbeth enters.

Macbeth	The cry is still they come.
	I have almost forgot the taste of fears.

Macbeth exits. Malcolm and Macduff make sudden strong attacking movements still concealed behind their branches. Hecate sees them.

Hecate	My lord, as I did stand my watch upon the hill, I looked towards
	Birnam, and anon. . .
Macbeth	Well, say sir.
Hecate	. . . methought the wood began to move.
Macbeth	Liar and slave.
Hecate	Let me endure your wrath, if't be not so.
	Fear not till Birnam Wood
	Do come to Dunsinane.
Macbeth	And now a wood comest to Dunsinane.
	Ring the alarum bell, blow wind, come wrack,
	At least we'll die with harness on our back.

Malcolm discards his branch. Macbeth moves threateningly towards him. Malcolm backs off. Macduff discards his branch.

Macduff	Turn hell-hound, turn.
Macbeth	Of all men else I have avoided thee: But get back, my soul is too much charg'd With blood of thine already.
Macduff	I have no words, My voice is in my sword.

They fight, using the bodhrans as shields. They beat them to represent blows. Macbeth suddenly retreats and Macduff waits.

Macduff	Yield thee coward.
Macbeth	I will not yield To kiss the ground before young Malcolm's feet.

Macbeth is suddenly distracted by Hecate who stands on a rostrum in a corner, watching the fight. She is taunting him.

Hecate	Macbeth shall never vanquished be Till great Birnam Wood to high Dunsinane Hill Shall come against him.
Macbeth	And now a wood do come to Dunsinane.
Hecate	Beware Macduff, beware the Thane of Fife.
Macbeth	And thou opposed being -
Hecate	Macduff, the Thane of Fife.
Macbeth	Before my body I throw my warlike shield. Lay on Macduff: And damned be him that first cries, 'Hold, enough.'

They fight and Macbeth is killed. Macduff lifts the crown high.

Macduff	Behold the usurper's cursed head. The time is free.

Drumming. Macduff takes crown to Malcolm who stands on the throne. Malcolm takes the crown. He puts it on his head.

Macduff	Hail, King of Scotland.

In the following silence, Malcolm sings very faintly one line of, 'I'm King of the Castle'. There is a pause, with everyone still. The actors unfreeze and beat the same rhythm on the bodhrans as they did at the beginning. The violin appears and plays the tune as the actors move about on the stage putting the throne in the centre with the crown on and the plaids of the main characters on the floor stemming from it. They circle the throne and then the music stops suddenly and the actors face the audience on all sides. They bow and exit, leaving the crown and plaids on stage.

Index